Time for Curriculum

Time for Curriculum

How School Board Members Should Think about Curriculum

What School Board Members Should Do about Curriculum

Henry M. Brickell
and
Regina H. Paul

Published by
The National School Boards Association, Alexandria, VA
and Teach 'em, Inc., Chicago, IL

Library of Congress Catalog Card Number:
87–51187

International Standard Book Number:
0–931028–98–1

Teach 'em, Inc.
160 East Illinois Street
Chicago, Illinois 60611

National School Boards Association
1680 Duke Street
Alexandria, Virginia 22314

92   91   90   89   88   5   4   3   2   1

Printed in the United States of America

To

Raymond L. Collins
Superintendent of the Manhasset Public Schools
Manhasset, New York
1945–1971

Contents

DEDICATION

This book is written for public school board members, but dedicated to public school teachers. Not to all public school teachers, but to those teachers who make a real difference in the lives of their students, who give their students a lasting impression of what high standards are and how to reach them. We dedicate this effort to improve elementary and secondary school curriculum to those teachers, knowing that they would applaud any effort to improve things—even though they themselves are already doing a fine job. That's the kind of teachers they are.

We want to thank a few in our own lives:

William S. Brubaker, whose junior high school social studies lectures gave students a preview of what was in store for them from the best college professors and whose charm let him get away with saying, "Life isn't fair. Why should I be?"

—R.H.P.

Laura Luker, whose junior high school science projects led her students across the boundary of the world they had known and into worlds vast and miniscule, sailing the universe in a classroom 24′ by 30′, Miss Luker at the helm and our noses pressed hard against the windows.

—H.M.B.

Leonard G. Murphy, whose junior high school instrumental music program was innovative and challenging and whose genuine caring for his students was never doubted by any young musician (even the tone-deaf ones).

—R.H.P.

Octavia Niehiesel, whose kindergarteners would jump through literal and figurative hoops to please her. May her wooden stick horses still prance in heaven for the preschool angels.

—H.M.B.

Agnes M. Raycroft, whose high school English classes kept the brightest students on their toes and whose insistence on perfection is what's missing from most classrooms. (You won't see any "possessive before the gerund" mistakes in this book.)

—R.H.P.

Peter C. Schmidt, whose high school English classes were a showcase of teaching techniques inside a little shop of horrors and whose personal interest in his students was sunshine splashing inside the cold gray walls.

—H.M.B.

ACKNOWLEDGMENTS

We owe a great deal to the school districts where we have worked in the past decade to develop the ideas presented in this book. They bravely let us try out things that were new and controversial—things that caused their teachers, their administrators, and even their school board members to be more accountable to each other and to the public.

There were many districts; we can't name them all. But here are those we are particularly indebted to. Some of them made enormous changes in the way they built curriculum and in the way they used it in the classrooms. It wasn't easy.

Bemidji Public Schools
Bemidji, Minnesota

School District of Brown Deer
Brown Deer, Wisconsin

Cleveland Public Schools
Cleveland, Ohio

Littleton Public Schools
Littleton, Colorado

Plainfield Public Schools
Plainfield, Connecticut

Richmond Public Schools
Richmond, Virginia

Riverhead Central School District
Riverhead, New York

Savannah-Chatham County Public Schools
Savannah, Georgia

Sonoma County Consortium
Sonoma County, California

- Cloverdale Unified School District
- Cotati-Rohnert Park Unified School District
- Geyserville Unified School District

Township High School District No. 211
Palatine, Illinois

Valley View Public Schools
Valley View, Illinois

In addition, there are many professionals who have worked with us to perfect our ideas and use them in the trenches. Some of those individuals who have been especially important to us and deserve our heartfelt thanks are:

Jerry Abbott, whose relentless pursuit of what a curriculum should ideally be gave his district a program that is very hard to match

Phil Bain, whose unshakable manner and clear intelligence have kept his district moving forward along the right track

Clint Barter, whose unusual daring moved a district ahead faster than most people would have thought possible

Jim Cole, whose genuine interest in and active pursuit of current professional thinking on key educational issues make him an asset to any district

Sue Cox, whose unfailing common sense has gotten her district through countless tight spots in a most ambitious curriculum overhaul

Pauline Davis, whose good-natured, but uncompromising, insistence gave her district its first-ever reading program with teeth in it—plus unsurpassed parent materials

Ron Etheridge, whose extraordinary vision and single-mindedness have transformed his district into a place where children are expected to learn—and do

Wanda Green, whose aggressive loyalty to the promise of education for all children—black and white—is far too rare today

Faith Hamre, whose clearheaded toughness keeps her unerringly on the side of educational improvement

Roger Lulow, whose easy intelligence solved tremendous problems in a district that most people had given up on

Pat Mathews, whose superb judgment and careful attention to detail have benefited school district after school district

David Pankake, whose wisdom in administering schools cannot be matched

Manny Scrofani, whose energy, ingenuity, and dedication to the proposition that things can be made better make him a remarkable administrator

Mary Shank, whose consistent support helped her district cope with the upheaval of curriculum improvement

Don Waldrip, whose plain-spoken determination made great changes possible in a district that faced all manner of obstacles

Finally, several organizations have given us marvelous opportunities to refine our ideas by presenting them to thousands of school board members and administrators at conferences of all kinds. For those platforms, we are indebted to the:

- National School Boards Association

- American Association of School Administrators

- Association for Supervision and Curriculum Development

- Danforth Foundation

Time for Civilians

The most remarkable thing about our remarkable country is this: Ordinary citizens control almost every major institution, public and private. No matter how many expert professionals are on the payroll, they do not have the last word. Somewhere above them, above the top of the pyramid of administrators (who do not have the last word either), is a group of civilians. They have the last word. They are not as expert as the experts, but they have the last word. They may know less about the operations than anyone on the payroll. Still, they have the last word.

Does this make sense? What it makes is democracy. Does that make sense? Government of the people, by the people, for the people. We, the people, govern ourselves. The professional experts do not govern us. We govern them; they serve us.

That is a particularly American idea. It may be the most American idea of all. No nation uses it more. It is our favorite form of governance. We use it for villages, townships, cities, counties, states, regions, the nation. We use it for sewers, police, roads, firefighting, rivers, libraries, airlines, prisons, forests, the military—every government function, without exception; all staffed by experts, without exception; and all governed by civilians.

Every government worker can say:

"The people who run this place know less about it than I do."

And we can say:

"That's right. The mayor knows less about police work than a detective does, and the city council knows even less. The governor knows less about the state universities than the professors do, and the legislature knows even less. The president knows less about the Air Force than the colonels do, and the Congress knows even less. Good thing.

"We wouldn't want your agency run by people who know as much about it as you do. We want it run by people who know less about it. Your problem is that you know too much. You are an expert, an insider. If you were in charge, you might run the place for the benefit of the insiders. We want the place run by outsiders. We want government of the outsiders, by the outsiders, for the benefit of the outsiders. We do not want government of the insiders, by the insiders, for the benefit of the insiders. That would be un-American. If you don't like that idea, you might try another country. You can leave here and travel in any direction, except north, and find plenty of them.

"Government of the outsiders, by the insiders, for the benefit of the insiders is extremely popular today, just as it has been throughout history. From the beginning of time, it has been almost every society's idea of how to govern. It's just not ours. So we're glad the people who run your government agency know less about it than you do. That means democracy is alive and well."

Americans like the idea of outsiders governing insiders so much, and we make it work so well inside the government, that we use it outside the government. We use it for churches—most of them, anyway. A board of civilian members of the congregation governs the professional staff, even though every member of the board knows less about church work than any member of the staff. We use it for the Red Cross and the Girl Scouts and the American Cancer Society and the Special Olympics— every one with a professional staff governed by civilians. We use it for private museums, private symphony orchestras, and private schools. You can stand among the experts in almost any organization and look up high enough and see a band of civilians looking down. In fact, you can stand inside almost any corporation, shoulder to shoulder with its experts, and look up to see an unqualified board of civilians at the top. Well, unqualified to be insiders, most of them, but qualified to be outsiders— qualified to run the place for the benefit of outside stockholders like themselves, placed there precisely to prevent the company from being run by insiders for the benefit of insiders. We don't like "insider trading" even in a private stock brokerage firm because it is bad for "outsider trading"—good for the employees, but bad for the customers.

We don't want insiders on the governing board, much as they might want to be there. Nobody understands this better than the top executive who works for the board. Ask any senior minister, hospital administrator, or museum director, "Who makes the worst board members?" They will tell you, "Another minister, another hospital administrator, another museum director."

Why do all top insiders want nothing but outsiders on the board of governors? Insiders make bad governors because they focus on the operations; outsiders make good governors because they focus on the results. Insiders prefer certain operations. Because they know so much, they develop strong opinions about *how* things should be done. Outsiders do not know enough to prefer certain operations. They may not even care about the operations. The consequence is that insiders on the board tend to judge the institution by its operations; outsiders on the board tend to judge the institution by its results.

Good chief executives want to be judged by their results. This gives them a weak allegiance to current operations. They are willing to change their operations in any way necessary to get good results. In this respect, they think like good board members, an essential job skill for any chief executive: Talk like an expert, think like a board member.

The preference of insiders for certain operations may result in pervasive bad effects if they become board members:

- They pull operational matters up onto the board agenda, where they don't belong.

- They argue eyeball to eyeball with the chief executive about operations: one expert versus another expert.

- They press the chief executive between board meetings to recommend certain operations they favor.

- They are too much interested in personnel matters, too little in everything else.

- They are excessively sympathetic toward employees—their wants, their opinions, their grievances—and too subject to pressure from employees.

- They make common cause with employees who prefer the same operations they prefer.

- They care about case-by-case decisions: who gets what job; which brand of equipment gets bought; which fringe benefits go into the negotiated package.

In short, they can defeat democratic governance by assisting the other inside experts to become self-governing.

Perhaps you are wondering whether any of this applies to schools. All of it does. The point is this: *Because* you are a civilian rather than an expert in education, you are qualified to govern the public schools.

Curriculum Is Too Complex for Civilians— Or Is It?

Curriculum is not as complex for a civilian member of a school board as medicine is for a civilian member of a hospital board.

But curriculum is complex. It is not so complex as medicine. But it is more complex than school transportation, more than school insurance, more than school building maintenance, more than school tax rates.

Curriculum is so complex that school board members tend to leave it to the educators, just as hospital board members tend to leave medicine to the doctors. That is too bad, because curriculum is more important than transportation, insurance, maintenance, and tax rates. It might be all right for school board members to leave the other matters to the educators, but not curriculum. School board members should control curriculum.

Now, you may not feel qualified. You may feel as unqualified to control curriculum as a hospital board member feels unqualified to control medicine. Nonetheless, you realize that medicine is the major business of hospitals—not ambulances, insurance, buildings, or charges to patients. And you realize that curriculum is the major business of schools—not transportation, insurance, buildings, or tax rates. Hospital board members may be satisfied to control the minor business of hospitals. But school board members must not be satisfied to control the minor business of schools. You must control the major business: curriculum.

When you finish this book, you will feel qualified.

A Curriculum Clock

Imagine the face of a clock—no, not a new-fashioned digital clock, but an old-fashioned round clock. This will be our curriculum clock. It will also be the table of contents for this book.

We'll go around the clock once quickly, as an overview of the theory behind the book. Then, we'll go around again slowly, with live illustrations of the theory at work in real school districts.

12:00—Selecting Goals and Objectives

Start at 12:00, the natural starting point on a clock, by setting goals and objectives. *Goals* are the big ones. *Objectives* are the little ones. The goals contain the objectives; the objectives spell out the goals.

The goals and objectives describe what you want to accomplish. If you were the board of a hospital, they would be about patient health. If you were the board of a church, they would be about the spiritual life of the congregation. If you were the board of the Boy Scouts, they would be about the character and skills of the boys. If you were the board of a social agency for the homeless, they would be about the physical and psychological well-being of the homeless people you served. If you were the board of a corporation, they would be about profits.

But you are the board of the public schools. Therefore, they will be about the thinking, feeling, and physical skills of public school students. They will be a description of the students you *imagine*. Putting it another way, they will be a description of the students you *plan*.

Goals sound like this:

- Reads and writes a foreign language
- Is skillful in using science lab equipment
- Shows pride in his or her work
- Judges works of art for style and technical quality
- Interprets graphs, charts, and tables
- Has skills useful in a variety of jobs
- Knows the history of his or her state
- Compromises with others to settle disagreements

Objectives sound like this:

- Identifies three services provided by local government
- Differentiates among complete sentences, fragments, and run-ons
- Rounds numbers to the nearest million, ten million, hundred million, billion, ten billion, or hundred billion
- Enjoys watching animals in their natural habitats
- Uses indirect objects in sentences
- Finds simple interest, using the formula $i = prt$
- Discusses factually both sides of the nuclear power controversy
- Evaluates the success of national and local muckrakers and reformers in getting legislation passed in the early 20th century in the United States
- Analyzes a poet's style, using three of his or her poems
- Labels a diagram of a dissected earthworm

No Other Goals and Objectives, Except Learning.
According to this clock, you cannot put anything at 12:00
except a description of how the students should come
out. The clock says that:

- It is not a goal to open an elementary school next fall.
- It is not an objective to adopt new science textbooks this spring.
- It is not a goal to raise teacher morale.
- It is not an objective to establish a new busing plan for better racial integration.
- It is not a goal to refinish the gymnasium floor before the basketball season opens.
- It is not an objective to introduce mastery teaching into the middle schools.
- It is not a goal to involve more parents in more school activities.
- It is not an objective to get a higher interest rate on the school district's money.

How would you feel if you opened an elementary
school next fall, but your students could not spell? How
would you feel if you raised teacher morale, but your students could not add or subtract? You would not feel satisfied. That's how you know that opening schools and
raising teacher morale and all the rest are not your goals.
You do those things only because you think they will help
get your goals accomplished, because they will help students spell, add, subtract, and all the rest.

12:00 Goals and Objectives Are the Planned ENDS.
What the board puts at 12:00 are the ENDS you plan to

accomplish. The clock says:

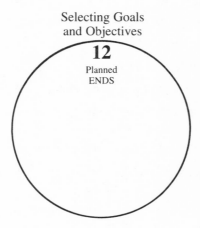

3:00—Selecting Programs

Move to 3:00. How will the goals and objectives you selected at 12:00 be accomplished? By the programs selected at 3:00.

The word "program" is professional educators' jargon for some combination of things needed to accomplish the goals and objectives. The combination is like a recipe; the things are like the ingredients.

Here are the ingredients of a program, listed in order of importance:

1. *Teachers.* Nothing is as important as who the teachers are—their intelligence, their personalities, their education, their affection for their students, their affection for their subjects, and their expectations of their students.

2. *Parents.* Next in importance are the parents of the students—their belief in the importance of schooling, their expectations for how their children will perform in school, and what they teach their children themselves, directly or indirectly.

3. *Times.* How long do teachers and parents spend teaching—in a day, in a week, in a month, in a year? Next to who the teachers are and who the parents are, the amount of time they spend teaching is most important.

4. *Materials.* Following the time schedule come the materials used for teaching the students—materials like textbooks, drapery fabric, workbooks, films, and flour; and equipment like tractors, kindergarten blocks, welding torches, clarinets, and stoves.

5. *Methods.* Surprisingly enough, less important than teachers, parents, times, and materials are the methods teachers and parents use during those times with those materials. The methods include lectures, demonstrations, discussions, homework, trips, projects, memory drills, and so on.

6. *Places.* Least important of all is where the teaching takes place—the school buildings, the classrooms, the libraries, the laboratories, the gymnasiums, the athletic fields, and of course the dining rooms and the kitchens and the living rooms of the children's homes.

A plan for a program is a plan for using these six ingredients in some mixture—a mixture of teachers and parents and times and materials and methods and places that someone thinks will cause the students to learn what they are supposed to learn. Just as a recipe is a plan for a casserole or a blueprint is a plan for a house, 3:00 is a plan for a program.

3:00 Programs Are the Planned MEANS. If 12:00 is the planned ENDS (the planned students or the planned learning), then 3:00 is the planned MEANS (the planned program or the planned teaching). In other words, 3:00 is what somebody imagines it would take to produce the 12:00 students you imagined you wanted.

You can see already that if you don't get the program planned at 3:00, then you won't get the students you planned at 12:00. The clock says:

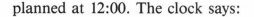

Selecting Goals
and Objectives

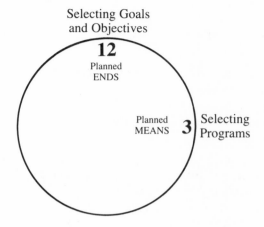

12

Planned
ENDS

Planned   **3** Selecting
MEANS   Programs

6:00—Operating Programs

Move to 6:00. Here the programs imagined at 3:00 are actually operated. If 3:00 is the planned teaching, 6:00 is the actual teaching. At 6:00, the actual teachers and the actual parents spend the actual time with the students using the actual materials and the actual methods in the actual places.

Unfortunately, as we said, the actual 6:00 may not match the ideal 3:00. Schools suffer many breakdowns around 4:30 on the clock. What was planned at 3:00 does not happen at 6:00. Teachers don't act the way they were supposed to, and parents don't, either. Time doesn't get used the way it was intended, and the materials don't, either. The methods actually used don't exactly match the methods called for in the 3:00 recipe. And the places in which teaching occurs may be less than the 3:00 ideal.

In other words, 3:00 is the paper description of the ideal; 6:00 is not paper, but people. The people don't exactly follow the paper, just as the cook does not exactly follow the recipe and the contractor does not exactly follow the blueprint. Open the typical classroom door and what you see the teacher doing with the students is not exactly what you meant. Open the typical apartment door and what you see the parents doing with their children is not exactly what you meant, either.

6:00 Programs Are the Actual MEANS. If 3:00 is the planned MEANS, then 6:00 is the actual MEANS. If 3:00 is the schools you should run, 6:00 is the schools you do run. Just as in life, sometimes things go better than planned, but usually they go worse.

And so, because the actual 6:00 program does not match the imagined 3:00 program, the goals and objectives you actually accomplish at 9:00 will not be the ones you imagined at 12:00. Just how far off the mark they are won't become clear until we move the clock hand to 9:00. The clock says:

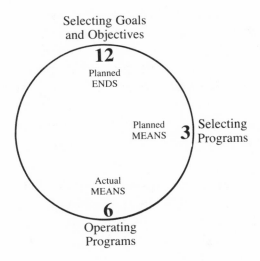

9:00—Measuring Goals and Objectives

Move to 9:00. Here you measure how well the goals and objectives were accomplished. What you measure at 9:00 is exactly what you called for at 12:00. The reason is that you want to compare what you got with what you asked for. You want to compare the actual 9:00 goals and objectives students did learn with the ideal 12:00 goals and objectives you hoped students would learn—the students you actually produced with the students you meant to produce.

Judging What You Cannot Measure. You cannot *measure* all of the things you want students to be able to think and feel and do. You can measure their spelling, their calculus, their rope climbing, their astronomy, their U.S. geography, and their typing. But you will have to *judge* their essays, their trombone blowing, their acting, their cooking, their watercolors and sculptures, their diving, and their lab notebooks. Of course, you want the judging to be as accurate, as fair, and as trustworthy as the measuring. That is because what must be judged is just as important as what can be measured.

There are many *measuring devices:* national tests, state tests, local tests, and so on. Some of these are paper-and-pencil tests, and some of them are performance tests. There are many *judging techniques:* rating scales, sample products, panels of experts, employers' opinions of graduates, and so on. You use those techniques for judging student products and student performances that cannot be measured.

9:00 Goals and Objectives Are the Actual ENDS. If 6:00 is the actual MEANS, then 9:00 is the actual ENDS. This is where you get the evidence of the goals and objectives that your students actually learned, the ENDS you actually achieved. The clock says:

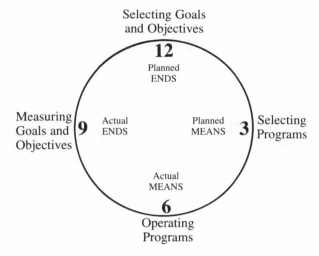

10:30—Setting Standards

You close the circle by comparing 9:00 to 12:00, completing the trip around the clock. Comparing the students you got to the students you wanted is *evaluation*. This is the most important act you will ever undertake as a board.

Despite what you have been told, this act is far more important than the act of appointing the superintendent. Why is that? Because this act will tell you whether you appointed the *right* superintendent. Putting it differently, the reason you appoint a superintendent in the first place is because you want someone who can make the actual 9:00 students match the ideal 12:00 students just as closely as possible. Boards have many criteria for selecting a superintendent. Without question, the most important criterion is whether the superintendent can make the 9:00 and 12:00 students match.

Let's say that evaluation takes place at 10:30, halfway between 9:00 and 12:00. But you cannot make that 10:30 evaluation unless you have *standards*. You have to answer the question: How high is up? How well do the students have to think at 9:00 for them to match the students you imagined at 12:00? How intensely do they have to feel? How skillfully do they have to move?

If you cannot answer those questions at 10:30, you cannot compare 9:00 to 12:00. That means you cannot evaluate how well you have accomplished your goals and objectives. Consequently, you cannot evaluate the success of the superintendent, and you cannot evaluate the success of the board. After all, you have only one purpose: the learning of the students. For that reason, the only way to evaluate your work as a board is to see whether you have accomplished that purpose, whether the actual 9:00 students match the ideal 12:00 students. There is no other way to judge your work as a board. The clock says:

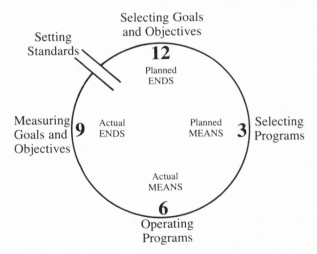

A Clock for All Times

This curriculum clock is universal. It can be used to think about any grade, any subject, any course, any lesson.

Take a grade—say, grade 4. At 12:00, the grade 4 goals and objectives are selected; at 3:00, the grade 4 programs to be used in teaching those goals and objectives are selected; at 6:00, the grade 4 programs are operated; at 9:00, the grade 4 goals and objectives are measured; and at 10:30, the actual 9:00 grade 4 learning is compared to the ideal 12:00 grade 4 learning, using the standards you set.

Take a lesson—say, a 30-minute lesson on the Louisiana Purchase. At 12:00, the lesson objectives are selected; at 3:00, the lesson teaching techniques (programs) are selected; at 6:00, the lesson is taught with those techniques; at 9:00, what the students have learned about the Louisiana Purchase is measured; and at 10:30, the learning obtained is compared to the learning wanted, using the standards you set.

Take any subject, such as French; or any course, such as French II; or any semester of French II; or any 45-minute period of French II. The curriculum clock applies equally to each one.

That's a powerful clock. You can use it to control any grade, any subject, any course, any lesson. You can use it to control what students learn during kindergarten, and you can use it to control what students learn between kindergarten and high school graduation.

Dividing the Work of the Board from the Work of the Superintendent

No decision you will ever make is more difficult than deciding what the board should do versus what the professionals should do. That is always difficult, no matter what the topic, and it is sometimes the cause of controversy between the board and the superintendent. Dividing the work in curriculum is the most difficult decision of all. It is, of course, the most important decision the board will ever make. Happily, the curriculum clock can sharpen your thinking before you decide, and it can stand as a clear record after you decide.

The way to think about dividing the territory between the board and the professionals is to remember
that 50,000 decisions about teaching and learning are
made in your school system every day school is in
session—or 500,000 if you are the board in a large school
system. You do not make any of them. Well, you make
very few of them. Even if you hold a meeting that very
day and make as many as five or ten decisions about
teaching and learning, that is a tiny fraction of all the
teaching and learning decisions that were made. The only
way to be in charge, the only way to govern, is to make
the most *important* ones.

Look at the face of the clock. What are the most important decisions: selecting 12:00 goals and objectives, selecting 3:00 programs, operating 6:00 programs,
measuring 9:00 goals and objectives, or setting 10:30
standards? Which decisions are most likely to put you in
charge? Which decisions, if you could make them, would
virtually dictate the other decisions? Which ones do you
care so much about that, if you could make those, someone else could make the others?

We have asked thousands of school board members
that same question: What do you want to control if you
cannot control everything? Most board members say they
would rather control learning than control teaching. They
say that if they could decide at 12:00 what students
should learn and at 9:00 what they have learned and at
10:30 whether they have learned it well enough, they
would let the superintendent and the professional staff
make the decisions about teaching. They say they would
strike this bargain with the superintendent and the professional staff: Draw a diagonal line between 1:30 and
7:30 on the curriculum clock; let the board control the
top half—12:00, 9:00, and 10:30; let the superintendent
and the professional staff control the bottom half—3:00
and 6:00. In fact, let the diagonal line be a fence dividing

the curriculum work of the board from the curriculum work of the professionals. Board members will agree not to jump the fence into professional territory if professionals will agree not to jump the fence into board territory.

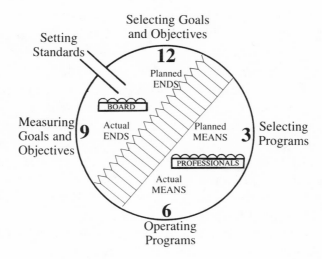

Make the fence about three feet high—low enough to see over and talk over, but high enough not to stumble over by accident or jump over on purpose. That way, the board room can be set up so that it straddles the fence, with board members sitting on one side and professionals on the other.

Board members can pass advice across the fence about what 3:00 programs to select as recipes or blueprints as well as advice about how to operate those programs at 6:00. But that advice from board members should be labeled clearly as *advice*. Likewise, professionals can pass advice across the fence at 12:00 about what students should be taught to think and feel and do, as well as advice at 9:00 about what the board should take as proof that the students can in fact do those things, as well as advice at 10:30 about how high to set the standards.

But that advice from the professionals should be labeled clearly as *advice*.

Of course, the professionals should agree to listen carefully to the advice from board members, and board members should agree to listen attentively to the advice from professionals. The diagonal fence is not intended to stop the shifting of *advice* back and forth between board members and professionals. It is intended to stop the shifting of *power*. The fence does not divide the information; it divides the control. Both parties can share the information, but they have to divide the control. The fence is designed to determine who has the ultimate power— who is finally in control—a very useful thing to know in case of disagreement between board members and professionals about curriculum.

You should expect disagreement. Board members will disagree with each other, professionals will disagree with each other, and board members and professionals will disagree with each other. What students should learn is debatable; how they should be taught is equally debatable. The debate is healthy. Not all goals can be taught; not all programs can be used. Have the debate. May the best goals win and may the best programs win. But let the board members pick the winning goals and let the professionals pick the winning programs.

Civilians Are Better Than Professionals at Selecting Goals, Deciding What To Accept as Proof of Learning, and Setting Standards

Over the years, the people who move through the seats on the school board will represent the general experience and the best values of the community. Board members will be exposed to the winds of public opinion and the waves of parental pressure and—once they come through the board room doors windblown and dripping and have a little time to shake themselves off—will winnow out from all of the many possibilities what is most important for students to learn and what is the best proof that they have learned it.

Of course, you as a board member will not write the 12:00 goals and you will not develop the 9:00 devices for measuring and judging and you will not dream up the 10:30 standards. What you will do is select them from among those proposed by the superintendent. That is, the professional staff will propose alternative things students could learn, and the board will decide what they should learn. Similarly, the professional staff will propose alternative methods of measuring and judging what students have learned, and the board will decide which of those methods would yield the most convincing proof. In the same fashion, the professional staff will propose the standards for deciding whether students have learned as much as they should, and the board will decide whether those standards are satisfactory—too low, too high, or just right. In short, you as a board member will not *do* the work at 12:00 or 9:00 or 10:30; you will simply *judge* the work. That is how you will control those points on the clock.

Professionals Are Better Than Civilians at Selecting Programs and Making Them Work

Unlike board members, professional educators live indoors most of the time. They are in schoolhouses all day teaching and are often in their own houses at night studying or grading papers or planning lessons. They are not so exposed to the winds and waves of community feeling as board members are. Thus, they are not so qualified to make decisions above the diagonal fence.

What professional educators are best at, what they are trained to do, what they do all day and half the night is to sift through alternative possible programs, select the most promising, and carry them out. They are experts in planning teaching and in doing teaching. Remember: The professionals have degrees in education. Most of their education courses dealt with alternative ways of teaching. It was their non-education courses—history, mathematics, astronomy, music, French, and so on—that contained what students might be taught to think and feel and be able to do.

Professional educators are, in short, trained as experts in MEANS, not as experts in ENDS. They think a great deal about MEANS, and they care a great deal about MEANS. In contrast, you as a board member are not trained in the MEANS of education. You do not know much about MEANS, you do not think much about MEANS, and you do not even care much about MEANS. That is why the diagonal fence assigns the control of learning to you and the control of teaching to the professional staff.

Your Clock Is Ticking

You already have a curriculum clock for your schools, whether you know it or not, ticking away 1,000 hours a year for each student. But you may not know what makes it tick or who is setting the hands or winding it up or letting it run down. In fact, some boards never even look at the face of the clock. They never know what time it is in the curriculum. But you should know. You should set the hands on the curriculum clock, wind it up, and watch the face. That is what it means to control the curriculum.

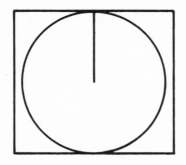

12:00   Selecting Goals and Objectives

Selecting Goals

There are all kinds of goals in life: sales quotas, election ambitions, market shares, military objectives, membership drives, financial targets, research objectives, fund-raising projections, win-loss hopes, Olympic records—all kinds. But a *curriculum goal* is something a student can learn in school.

Three Categories of Goals

Educators agree that there are three categories of learning:

- Cognitive
- Affective
- Psychomotor

Blame the educational psychologists for those names. But the psychologists' names for those categories don't matter.

Happily for the English language, the 4-H Clubs had already figured out what students could learn and had made the same list in plain words—long before the psychologists got around to it. The 4-H Clubs list read:

- Head
- Heart

- Hand
- Health

If the 4-H Clubs had wanted to be the "3-H" Clubs, we would have had a perfect match:

Psychologists	*"3-H" Clubs*
Cognitive	Head
Affective	Heart
Psychomotor	Hand

But the Clubs threw in *Health* for a fourth *H*. It shows their good sense.

The fourth *H* is the result of having the first three. That is, a person with a well-educated head, a well-educated heart, and a well-educated hand will most likely turn out to be mentally healthy, emotionally healthy, and physically healthy. Or, to put it a different way, you don't educate the health. You educate the head, the heart, the hand—and the health results. So the psychologists and the 4-H Clubs agree perfectly after all: There are three categories of *learning*.

Professional educators have different names for the same three categories. And then there are the common sense names board members use:

Psychologists	*4-H Clubs*	*Educators*	*Board Members*
Cognitive	Head	Knowledge	Thinking
Affective	Heart	Attitudes	Feeling
Psychomotor	Hand	Skills	Doing

It doesn't matter which names you use. We will probably use them all in this book. What does matter is this: Don't let yourselves get confused by the names. There may be 20 different names, but there are only three categories of learning.

All curriculum goals fit into one of the three categories. It doesn't matter what grade, and it doesn't matter what subject. Curriculum goals in the three categories are the stuff kindergarten and third grade and eighth grade and twelfth grade and all the other grades are made of. They are the stuff English, mathematics, science, social studies, foreign languages, art, music, physical education, home economics, welding, and all the other subjects are made of.

Curriculum goals go at 12:00 on the curriculum clock. Every 12:00 goal—without exception—names something a student can learn to know, to feel, or to do.

Some Sample Goals

Here are some sample goals that represent a variety of school subjects. Do you have goals like these at 12:00 in your school district?

- Operates a personal computer to perform tasks at school or home
- Obeys traffic regulations
- Analyzes and interprets literature
- Speaks fluently, distinctly, and expressively
- Has good health habits
- Knows how to complain about unsatisfactory goods and services
- Works safely around machinery
- Solves statistical problems
- Uses his or her skills in music, dance, drama, and/or visual arts for recreation
- Believes in good sportsmanship
- Thinks scientifically—hypothesizes, experiments, analyzes, and concludes

- Describes the economic systems of major nations
- Has enough office skills to get a job
- Thinks critically—selects information, sees patterns, and evaluates
- Knows how to apply and interview for a job
- Has good study habits
- Sets realistic personal goals
- Is skillful in group discussions
- Respects the rights and property of others

That's what we mean by goals. You will need about 100-150 to cover your priorities for students at 12:00.

Should You Select the Goals?

"Listen here, you two! I am a CPA, okay? I know my accounting. But you're asking me as a school board member to pick those curriculum goals. No way, my friends, no way. That's what we pay the superintendent and all his spear-carriers to do for us. I don't know enough, and my fellow board members don't know enough."

The man—an expert in his own field—was explaining his opinions to us. Do you agree with him? Can you as a school board member choose among these goals or should you turn the job over to the professional educators?

- Is it more important to teach students to speak a foreign language or to teach them to read great literature in a foreign language?
- Is it more important to teach students to know about drugs (for example, the names of illegal drugs and the penalties for using them) or to teach them to stay away from drugs, whatever their names and regardless of their penalties?

- Is it more important to teach students to love art or to teach them to do art?

- Is it more important to teach students to read well or to teach them to write well?

- Is it more important to teach students an entry-level job skill or to teach them how to look for a job?

If you either cannot answer such questions—or do not care about answering them—read no further. This book is for school board members who believe they know something about such choices, care about them, and insist that civilians should decide the relative importance of such learning goals. This book is for school board members who believe that decisions about what to teach students cannot be left in the hands of professional educators—each one of whom has his or her own special knowledge, special interests, special preferences, and special teaching abilities.

Remember: We are talking only about *what* to teach students, not *how* to teach students. *How* to teach them—what teachers, what scheduling, what materials, what methods, what places—is important, and we will talk about it at 3:00 on the curriculum clock. But here we are talking about *what* to teach them. If you believe—as we do—that your thoughts and your values and those of the taxpayers you represent must determine curriculum goals for students, read on.

Should You Decide Alone?

You can select curriculum goals as a school board, or you can do it after soliciting advice from others.

The arguments for doing it alone as a board are straightforward:

- You were elected to lead the people. The voters do not

expect you to ask their opinions at every fork in the road.

- Ask for advice and you might have to take it.

- People disagree about goals for the schools. The more people you ask, the more disagreement you will hear—or, worse yet, the more disagreement you will create.

- It is quicker to do it alone.

- It is cheaper to do it alone.

On the other hand, the arguments for soliciting advice are equally straightforward:

- These are the most important decisions that will ever be made in your school district.

- All stakeholders have a right to express their opinions on such important decisions—taxpayers, school staff members, even students.

- It is a great public relations exercise to ask people their opinions about important issues—even if you do not always take their advice.

- Involving all stakeholders in the selection of goals will help prevent them from taking potshots at the goals later.

- Soliciting advice from a wide range of stakeholders will help prevent board members from listening too closely to small, but vocal, special interest groups.

Virtually all school boards we have met make choice two—soliciting advice—for the reasons given. Whatever their reasons, most school boards learn a great deal from the advice they get—both things that they did not know before and things that they always knew, but could never prove.

Whom To Ask?

Ideally, all of those who have a stake in the school district's goals should be asked. Here is our list of stakeholders:

- *Community residents*—After all, they foot the bill. We don't mean just parents; nonparents pay taxes, too, and they make up roughly 75 percent of most communities.

- *School staff*—They are the professionals— administrators, teachers, specialists, counselors, librarians, and the rest. They know a great deal about what can be learned by students. And, if they don't want to teach what you order at 12:00, chances are it won't get taught.

- *High school students*—There is one thing you can say about high school students: If they don't want to learn something, they probably won't.

- *Recent high school graduates*—These are the individuals on the campuses, in the work places, and in the homes who are now trying to use what they learned in school. They know better than anyone else what is proving helpful and what is not.

How To Ask?

There are several ways to ask these four populations for advice on goals. One school board or another has tried them all. The methods include these:

- *Wait for advice; don't ask for it.* Just wait for those cards and letters to come in, for delegations to show up, for individuals to buttonhole board members or administrators, for your telephone to ring, for letters and editorials to appear in the newspapers. This method is easy to use, but it will yield lopsided advice,

not evenly representative of all four populations—
indeed, not *representative* of any one.

- *Sponsor meetings.* This takes more effort than waiting, and it will bring in more advice. However,
  whether these are held as open "hearings" or as invi-
  tational meetings with selected spokespersons, it is
  very hard to control the agenda, cover a large number
  of topics, collect opinions from the shy, and prevent
  mob psychology.

- *Appoint advisory committees.* This is probably the
  best method, short of a well-planned survey. You can
  select representative groups, give them ample time to
  deliberate, set their timetables, determine their re-
  porting formats, and probe for any further information you want after they finish.

- *Conduct a well-planned, systematic survey.* This is the
  best method—but, of course, the most expensive. The
  difficulties include developing a good questionnaire,
  administering it, and tabulating the answers. The advantages are that you can control the agenda, cover a lot
  of topics, get genuinely representative opinions (the biggest advantage), and interpret the results easily.

Because it is the best method for soliciting advice,
here are our ideas about how to conduct a well-planned,
systematic survey—based on our own experience in making such surveys for local school districts of all kinds and
sizes.

- If your community is relatively small—say, 5,000
  households or fewer—mail a questionnaire to every
  household. You will worry about the expense, but the
  public relations value of asking every household in
  town about the central purpose of schooling will become clearer and clearer to you as you all talk together as a board.

  If your community is larger than about 5,000 households, on the other hand, you will be forced to pick a small, scientifically adequate "random" or "systematic" sample of residents in order to keep the cost down.

Some Alternatives to Mail. Can you have the survey conducted during community meetings rather than by mail? Yes, you can, but you won't reach as many people and those you do reach will probably be a biased sample of the community. Can you have the survey conducted by telephone? Yes, you can, but you won't be able to reach as many people because it will be expensive to conduct (if you use a professional survey company) or time consuming to manage (if you recruit, train, and supervise volunteers). Can you have volunteers go door-to-door to deliver and collect a questionnaire from each household? Yes, you can, but you will need to put a lot of time and effort into recruiting those volunteers and managing their efforts.

In the end, mailing questionnaires to community residents usually turns out to be the best choice.

• Hand out questionnaires to school staff members and ask them to fill out questionnaires overnight or on school time. Have an administrator check off the returned questionnaires so that the missing ones can be chased.

• Mail the questionnaires to the last known addresses of graduates from one or two classes that finished high school no more than five years ago (18 months to two years ago is ideal). If graduates have been out of high school longer than that, too many addresses will be out of date. More important, the answers of the graduates will begin to look exactly like those of the community residents.

• Make sure your high school students fill out a questionnaire in class when they are a captive audience. If your high school population is quite large, pick one class for the survey (juniors are ideal). Use student representatives to explain and monitor the survey. They will be proud of their involvement, and you will be proud of the job they will do.

What Questions To Ask?

This is where you will make or break a goal survey. Surveys that ask the wrong questions cannot possibly give you the right answers. Here are the four most common mistakes we have seen in both popular commercially-produced questionnaires and homemade questionnaires:

Mistake #1.   *Learning goals hopelessly scrambled together with teaching processes, school operations, and indicators of school climate.* Making this mistake will result in a confusing ballot on which it is impossible to vote. Here is an excerpt similar to one commercially-published survey that makes this mistake:

Rank these topics according to how important each topic is for the schools to address:

____Reading

____Mathematics

____Discipline

____Education for the handicapped

____Reporting student progress

____Parent involvement in school activities

____Training students for jobs

____Computers

____Science

____Competitive athletics

____Foreign languages

____Moral and ethical behavior

The biggest problem with a competition like this is that it is really no competition at all. You do not have to trade discipline for reading. You do not have to trade mathematics for parent involvement in school activities. There is no reason why these topics should be entered into a horse race with each other.

However, you may well have to trade foreign languages for mathematics or art for science. That is the real competition, the competition over which you as a school board member must preside. Therefore, your goal survey must place only *learning goals* in the questionnaire when you ask for advice.

Mistake #2. *Learning goals too abstract to guide curriculum decisions*. Making this mistake will leave your curriculum director unable to make any sense out of the results. If you have people vote on the importance of broad topics such as citizenship, health, recreation and leisure, and basic skills—as one popular survey has people do—your curriculum director will not know what to tell the social studies teachers when they convene to refine and update your social studies curriculum. There is not enough information in such broad goal areas to help at 12:00.

Mistake #3. *Learning goals written only for the head and not for the heart or the hand*. Making this mistake will accidentally give you a curriculum with too much thinking and too little feeling and doing.

There is an assumption here that we had better check. Do you teach any attitudes in your school district? Do you want students to feel a certain way about anything—about democracy, about literature, about paintings, about physical fitness? Do you teach any physical skills in your school district? Do you want students to be able to do anything—make an omelette, handle laboratory equipment, play the violin, use a ruler?

Of course, you teach attitudes and physical skills like those. So you must be careful to give your community residents, school staff members, current high school students, and recent high school graduates the opportunity to vote on attitudes and skills like those. Some questionnaires forget that you—just like the 4-H Club

—teach the whole student. Don't forget attitudes and skills when it comes time to make up or choose your goal survey questionnaire.

Mistake #4.   *Learning goals chosen for their importance for students to learn rather than for their importance for schools to teach.* This is the biggest mistake of all. We learned this lesson from a parent in Wisconsin. When we were first developing our goal survey, we tried it out one afternoon with a roomful of parents. We had just handed out draft copies of the questionnaire when a woman in the back raised her hand.

"I can't answer your questionnaire," she said.

"Oh, no," we said. "What's wrong? Aren't the goals clearly written? Don't you understand them?"

"They're clear, all right," she replied. "But the questionnaire says: *How important is it for your child to learn this?* Now, you see the first goal? It's very important for my child to learn, but I don't want the schools to teach it. It's something I want to do at home with her. So, do I give it a high rating because it's very important for my child to learn or a low rating because I don't want you to do it in school?"

She had seen something we had missed.

Students learn in many places, as we all know. They learn at home, in Boy Scouts, in church youth groups, from television, at their after-school jobs, from their friends, and so on. Many things are extremely important for students to learn, but far less important for public schools to teach. Importance to learn is one thing; importance for schools to teach is another. You must separate those two topics in a goal survey. Otherwise, you will end up with an order too tall for the public schools to fill—and one that your stakeholders do not really expect the schools to fill in the first place.

Here is one learning goal we use in the Educational Goals Survey (EGS) we developed: "Has a satisfying hobby (stamp collecting, reading, crafts, etc.)."

That goal will typically get a rating of about *5* (on a scale from *0* to *7*) on importance for *students to learn*, but will get a rating of only about *3* on importance for *schools to teach*. In other words, it is important for students to have a hobby, but it is not important enough for schools to spend time during the short school day teaching it.

Only when you ask *both* questions can you differentiate the work of the schools from the work of the community. Without that differentiation, you will try to do everything—and you will not succeed.

Here are some characteristics of EGS (published by and available from the National School Boards Association) we have found to be useful in our work at 12:00 with school districts. Keep these in mind if you are making up your own questionnaire or if you are going to buy a commercially-published one:

- The EGS questionnaire contains 277 specific learning goals, which represent all 14 school subjects.

- These goals are divided up into four different questionnaires so that no one respondent has to answer questions about all 277, but rather answers one questionnaire containing only about 70 representative goals.

- The EGS goals are about 60 percent for the head (knowledge), 30 percent for the heart (attitudes), and 10 percent for the hand (physical skills).

- The EGS goals are specific enough to have clear curriculum implications. Here are a few more of the 277 (others were listed earlier in this book):

  - Knows what taxes pay for
  - Reads with understanding
  - Appreciates what different races, religions, and nationalities have contributed to American life
  - Computes accurately (adds, subtracts, multiplies, and divides)
  - Wants to take music, dance, drama, or art lessons

- Accepts responsibility for his or her own behavior
- Knows the effects of alcohol and tobacco
- Invents new approaches to difficult problems
- Plays on sports teams for recreation
- Writes correctly (proper grammar, punctuation, and capitalization)

- Three separate questions are asked about *each* of the 277:

  1. How important is it for *students to learn* (on a scale from *0* to *7*)?

  2. How important is it for *schools to teach* (on a scale from *0* to *7*)?

  3. Is it so important that it should be *required for graduation* —that is, no student should receive a high school diploma if he or she has not learned it (*yes* or *no*)?

- The 18 science goals are scattered throughout the four questionnaires, hidden among all the other goals like Easter eggs, so that the people who really love science must hunt down those 18 separate goals and rate each one a *7*. The 14 music goals are scattered the same way. So are all the goals in the remaining school subjects. This is the best form of measurement, because it gives you the best assurance that each goal was read and rated independently on its own merits.

- The EGS questionnaire does something else that is very unpleasant. It says:

  "Take $1,000 and spend it on the 14 school subjects to show the importance of each one. Don't consider how much it actually costs to teach each subject. Just spread around the $1,000 to show how much you value each subject."

Sometimes when we have the questionnaire completed in a group setting, someone will raise a hand and say something like:

  "I'm about halfway down the list, and I've noticed that there are some good subjects left in the bottom half.

> But, I've used up all my money. Could I have some more money?"

And we say:

> "Would you like your taxes raised in order to get more money?"

And what do you think the answer is? That's right.

> "No."

> Now, we know that $1,000 is too little money. This spending game puts the 14 school subjects in direct competition with each other for too little money. We tell people that this spending game puts them in the same predicament that school board members are in every day: There are many good things to teach students, but there is not enough money to teach them all. Someone has to choose. School board members are elected or appointed to make just those choices. The survey is one good opportunity for others to "play school board" and give their advice on what to do when you can't do everything.

On the following page is a sample page from the EGS questionnaires, showing 12 of the 277 goals and the questions we ask about each one. You can use it as a model for creating your own survey, or you can use it as a template for judging other commercially-produced surveys.

How To Analyze the Results?

You will want just these simple statistics:

- *For each goal,* an average (mean) rating of its importance for *students to learn* and, separately, of its importance for *schools to teach.*

- *For each school subject* as a whole, an average (mean) rating of its importance for *students to learn* and, sep-

Sample Survey Form

How important is each goal for students to learn (regardless of where they learn it—at home, through friends, in community youth organizations, from television)?

How important is each goal for schools to teach?

Is each goal so important that a student should not get a high school diploma if he or she had not learned it?

THE GRADUATING SENIOR...		How important is it for...		
		STUDENTS TO LEARN? Low Medium High (Circle)	SCHOOLS TO TEACH? Low Medium High (Circle)	Should it be REQUIRED for GRADUATION? (Circle)
	SAMPLE: Knows what action to take as a consumer when cheated	0 1 2 3 4 (5) 6 7	0 1 2 (3) 4 5 6 7	(NO) YES
1.	Knows the fundamental concepts of mathematics	0 1 2 3 4 5 6 7	0 1 2 3 4 5 6 7	NO YES
2.	Spells correctly	0 1 2 3 4 5 6 7	0 1 2 3 4 5 6 7	NO YES
3.	Reads with understanding	0 1 2 3 4 5 6 7	0 1 2 3 4 5 6 7	NO YES
4.	Wants to continue to learn throughout his/her life	0 ~~SAMPLE~~ 4 5 6 7	1 4 5 6 7	NO YES
5.	Has a satisfying hobby (stamp collecting, reading, crafts, etc.)	0 1 2 3 4 5 6 7	0 1 2 3 4 5 6 7	NO YES
6.	Names different means of transportation, reads schedules, and compares fares	0 1 2 3 4 5 6 7	0 1 2 3 4 5 6 7	NO YES
7.	Is skillful in using science lab equipment	0 1 2 3 4 5 6 7	0 1 2 3 4 5 6 7	NO YES
8.	Combines ideas in clever new ways	0 1 2 3 4 5 6 7	0 1 2 3 4 5 6 7	NO YES
9.	Maintains physical fitness through proper diet, exercise, and health habits	0 1 2 3 4 5 6 7	0 1 2 3 4 5 6 7	NO YES
10.	Has academic skills needed for further schooling	0 1 2 3 4 5 6 7	0 1 2 3 4 5 6 7	NO YES
11.	Speaks a second language	0 1 2 3 4 5 6 7	0 1 2 3 4 5 6 7	NO YES
12.	Knows United States history	0 1 2 3 4 5 6 7	0 1 2 3 4 5 6 7	NO YES

Form C

Copyright © 1981

⊙ There are about 265 more goals!

⊙⊙ There are 3 other forms!

arately, of its importance for *schools to teach*. This is the average (mean) rating of the ratings of all the goals that make up that school subject.

- *For each goal*, the percent of respondents who thought it should be *required for high school gradua-tion*.

- *For each school subject*, the average (mean) amount of money spent on it in the spending game.

You cannot produce these statistics until you decide one important thing: How much weight will you give to each population you surveyed? That is a matter for you to decide, but we recommend *one population = one vote*. Give them equal weight.

To be specific, you would take the averages (means) of the answers of community residents, school staff members, recent high school graduates, and current high school students. That would give you four numbers. You would add them up and divide by four, giving you an overall average for all four groups put together. We have already explained why each population's perspective on the question of what to teach students is uniquely valu-able and equally significant. Therefore, *one population = one vote*.

A Curriculum for the Community. When you ask both how important it is for *students to learn* and how important it is for *schools to teach* each goal, you can do a nifty bit of mathematics, using the following formula:

L - T = CC	L = Learning rating T = Teaching rating CC = Curriculum for the community rating

Translated, this formula means that if you subtract the *teaching* rating from the *learning* rating, you will get an indication of whether a goal would be a good candidate for the *curriculum for the community*.

Let's take an example. As we said earlier, if "Has a satisfying hobby" gets a rating of *5* on importance for *students to learn* and a rating of *3* on importance for *schools to teach*, the formula would work like this:

$$L - T = CC$$
$$5 - 3 = 2$$

If you apply that formula to all of the goals in your survey, the goals with a learning rating of at least *5* and a curriculum for the community rating of at least positive *1* will be your best candidates for a curriculum for the community. The survey respondents will have told you that these goals are important for students to learn, but far less important for schools to teach. The community should fill in that gap. Out of our EGS list of 277 goals, we usually get about 50 to 75 goals voted as good candidates for a curriculum for the community.

What would you do with such a curriculum? You would ask your superintendent to take it to his or her next meeting with the Chamber of Commerce, community religious leaders, youth organization heads, the PTA, and other groups serving young people and their families. Such groups are typically expected to teach students something outside of school hours. They are the ones to help you out once you get your priorities straight, admit that the schools can't do it all, and work out a curriculum for the community.

Your schools and your community might strike a kind of bargain: You will do certain things very well during school hours, and they will do certain other things very well outside of school hours. Neither of you can do it all, and neither of you should. That's what we usually find out when we survey a community.

What Will You Find Out?

The first thing you will probably find out is that people agree more often than they disagree. In surveys we have conducted, we have found that community residents, school staff members, current high school students, and recent high school graduates generally agree on what is important for schools to teach and what is not. That should be very reassuring to you and to your superintendent. It allows you to please the majority of the people the majority of the time.

The second thing you will probably find out is that people are very clear about what they want from the schools. They have no difficulty separating the schools' job from the community's job. In a nutshell, most people believe that the schools' main job is intellectual development, while the community's main job is character development. Most important, the schools cannot graduate students who have good characters, but poor intellects. That is a trade-off that your stakeholders will not allow the schools to make.

The third thing you will probably find out is that people are discriminating in choosing high school graduation requirements. Here is the standard we use: More than 50 percent of the community residents, more than 50 percent of the school staff members, more than 50 percent of current high school students, *and* more than 50

percent of the recent high school graduates must all agree
that a goal should become a high school graduation requirement before we would recommend that the board
adopt it. Of our 277 goals, the typical community will
vote between 15 and 30 into the winners' circle. It would
not surprise you if we told you that most of those winners
are reading, writing, and arithmetic, with a pinch of history, geography, civics, and biology thrown in.

What about Competition among the Subjects?

Let's take English and math as an example. Here is
something you already know: English, especially reading,
is the most important school subject. Right?

Wrong. Mathematics is surpassing English as the
most important subject—or it soon will. Even now, it is at
least tied with English in most surveys we have conducted.

Don't feel too bad if you didn't know that. Most audiences of school administrators we talk with don't know
it either. Then who does know? Most of your stakeholders—especially students. Current high school students consistently rate mathematics higher *relative* to English than any of the other three populations do. Can they
see the wave of the future better than school leaders can?

Indeed, the only *attitude* ever voted as a graduation
requirement by a majority of each of the four populations surveyed was: "Believes it is important to have good
mathematical skills." Feeling the right way about math is
evidently more important than feeling the right way
about anything else the goal survey offered—English, democracy, yourself, others, drugs, sex, and the other important items on the menu.

Are those stakeholders serious about this? We think

they are. Just as serious as when 98 percent of them typically vote "Computes accurately (adds, subtracts, multiplies, and divides)" as the number one graduation requirement.

Have you looked recently at what you require students to learn in math versus English? Do you know that elementary school teachers usually spend at least twice as much time on English as math? Do you let students opt out of math in high school sooner than you let them opt out of English? Most school districts do. Are you doing your job at 12:00?

What Is Most Important within Each Subject?

Just as you must judge the importance of each school subject, you must also judge what is most and least important *within* each school subject. Only then can your curriculum director, with the help of your teachers, break down the important goals into detailed curriculum objectives.

(Remember that each subject is represented by from 10 to 30 goals in the EGS questionnaire, thus allowing you to look *within* each subject to see what is most and least important.)

Here are a few examples of the specifics we have found in some of our surveys. If you do not know how your stakeholders feel about matters like these, you are not ready to judge what is most important and thus you are not ready to set curriculum goals.

Art and Music. Art and music are frequently voted as the *least* important subjects in the curriculum. Those of us who love the arts search hard in the survey results to see whether respondents think *any* of the goals within art and music are worth teaching. When we look inside art and music at the way each separate goal is rated, we find something intriguing.

Apparently, the art and music curricula in schools today are aimed in the wrong direction. What the community residents, school staff members, high school students, and recent graduates all want is "spectator" art and music. Not "varsity" art and music.

Goals like these top the art and music lists:

- Appreciates paintings, drawings, and sculptures

- Appreciates music

Goals like these fall to the bottom of the art and music lists:

- Paints, draws, or sculpts well

- Plays a musical instrument or sings well

Now, in your imagination, walk down the hall in one of your schools. Pick any grade. Open the door of the art or music room. What are the students doing? Are they drawing and painting? Are they blowing, bowing, and singing? Or are they looking at slides of Monet's *Water Lilies* and listening to Tchaikovsky's *Swan Lake*? Are they producing art and music or consuming it? They are producing it, aren't they—whether you picked grade 1, 4, 7, 9, or 12.

It is art and music appreciation—not production and performance—that people want. It is art and music production and performance—not appreciation—that they are getting.

The survey respondents are not saying that you should disband your orchestra or take down the exhibits at your spring art show. What they are saying is that art and music appreciation are for everyone (100 percent of your student body and 100 percent of the adult population), while art and music production are for a select, talented few (say, 10 percent of your student body and 1 percent of the adult population). Keep your orchestra and keep your art show, but don't let the "varsity" curricula that produced them be *the* art and music curricula for *all* your students.

As one superintendent in an East Coast state said to us recently:

> "No wonder no one complained when I cut the positions of 20 art teachers in our elementary schools. Looks like they weren't teaching what most people wanted."

Who is deciding what to teach in your art and music classrooms right now? You? Your superintendent? Your curriculum director? Your principals? Probably not. You—and your superintendent and your curriculum director and your principals, unfortunately—have probably turned the 12:00 art and music decision over to the 3:00 art and music teachers you hired. You are letting 3:00 dictate 12:00—exactly backwards.

What the art and music teachers are doing is making copies of themselves. You can't really blame them. They have been trained to produce art and music, and they believe students should be taught to produce it as well. They are performing artists, training young performing artists. (Some of them even believe that students cannot be taught to appreciate art and music *unless* they can produce it.)

If you had been serious about art and music appreciation at 12:00, you would have hired art historians, museum curators, and music critics at 3:00—people who know about and appreciate the arts. They would be making copies of themselves, training young spectators of the arts rather than training varsity violinists.

When was the last time your board met to consider your art and music goals? If you can't remember, you have not been doing your job at 12:00. But somebody else has: the band director—an inside expert.

Foreign Languages. Among the foreign language goals, we find that it is more important for students to appreciate and know about the *cultures* of foreign countries than it is for them to be able to read, write, speak, and listen in a foreign language. What is much *less* important than any of those skills is being able to read and interpret literature written in a foreign language. All four groups of respondents agree about that.

Maybe this does not seem too surprising. After all, if students ever travel abroad or happen to get a job calling for a foreign language, you can be assured that they will not be asked to read and interpret the literature native to that language.

That brings you to an interesting problem in your own schools. How many students do you have in your fourth-year foreign language program—say, French IV? How many students do you have in French I? Are the numbers the same? No. They are not the same in any school district in the country.

Here is one reason for the universal attrition between first and fourth year. What do you find when you look inside your fourth-year language program—and even your third-year program? Foreign language literature— and lots of it. Most students drop out of foreign language study as soon as it becomes a study of literature rather than a study of foreign cultures and the foreign language skills (reading, writing, speaking, and listening). A surprise? It shouldn't be. Community residents, school staff members, high school students, and recent graduates all agree that the study of foreign language literature is not very important. You are teaching something in the third and fourth years that no one values much.

Why are you doing that? Your teachers do not move on to literature because they have already made students proficient in cultural understanding and language skills in just two years; they couldn't do that in four years. Who decided on the 12:00 foreign language goals? You? Your superintendent? Your curriculum director? Your principals? Probably not. Again, you have let the 3:00 people you hired—the foreign language teachers—develop the 12:00 goals. You were running the clock backwards.

But why would foreign language teachers put unimportant goals at 12:00, thereby costing themselves enrollment in their upper-level courses and perhaps eventually costing themselves their jobs? In a national survey we did for the American Council on the Teaching of Foreign Languages (the professional association of language teachers), we asked foreign language teachers what their greatest weakness was. Too many of them said, "We cannot speak the language we teach." Now, think about what those teachers probably studied in at least their last two years of college in their foreign language major. What was it? That's right—literature.

The people you have allowed to determine the 12:00 foreign language goals are neither very good at speaking the languages nor very recently trained in anything but the literature of the languages. You really can't blame them for letting their own backgrounds and expertise determine their 12:00 curriculum.

But is it *their* 12:00 curriculum? No, it's yours. And you can be blamed for letting it get out of control. If you have not dealt with what's inside your foreign language courses, you have not been doing your job at 12:00. And the students—voting with their feet—are letting you know it.

Health. Where do you think health usually ranks in importance for *schools to teach* among the 14 school subjects? Let's make it easy. Would you say health ranks in the bottom half of the school subjects? Most people would—unless they had done a goal survey.

Actually, health frequently ranks *third* in importance —behind math and English, but ahead of everything else. Surprised? What in the world brings health nearly to the top of the survey list? Looking at the goals that make up health, we see what it is.

The goals that rate so well in health are those that teach students to *avoid* the "adult pleasures." You all know what those are: tobacco, alcohol, sex, and drugs—not necessarily in that order. Of those four adult pleasures, drugs are coming up more and more often in the surveys as the biggest problem—whether you ask community residents, school staff members, high school students, or recent graduates. They say it is more important for schools to teach students to "Believe illegal drugs are harmful" than to teach students to "Name illegal drugs and penalties for using them." What the respondents are calling for is a health curriculum for the heart, not the head. It is a curriculum of attitudes, not knowledge, that they want.

Perhaps avoiding sex will surpass avoiding drugs in the near future as the problems of teenage pregnancies and AIDS loom larger and larger. A curriculum director, playing tennis recently with the mother of a high school student, had this conversation:

"What's your idea of a good sex education curriculum?" he asked.

The mother replied, "That's easy. I can give it to you in four simple words: Tell my daughter, 'Don't.' "

Clarify her daughter's values about sex? Make sure her daughter thinks through her own values and comes to her own conclusions about sex? No.

Give her daughter the right values about sex. Tell her daughter:

"We don't drive drunk; we don't pick up live electrical wires; we don't do sex. Those things can hurt you. So don't do them."

Avoiding the adult pleasures is not a moral, ethical, or religious matter beyond the reach of the public schools. It is a matter of physical *health* and emotional *health*. It belongs in the school health curriculum and will make health a very important school subject, according to the people we have surveyed.

Have you looked inside your health curriculum lately? Are you teaching students things like good health habits and the importance of physical fitness, or are you teaching them things like attitudes for coping with the health problems that are getting worse in our society? Do you think you are satisfying your stakeholders when you teach students to clarify their values about drugs (whatever values they have are okay as long as they think hard about them) when you could have been teaching them the clear value that drugs are bad? Are you doing your job in health at 12:00?

Social Studies. We can tell you that social studies is slipping in importance in the curriculum. It frequently ranks below mathematics, English, and science. It is no longer keeping company with those other basic academic subjects. Did you already know that? Did you suspect it, but couldn't prove it?

What has happened to social studies? A look at the goals within social studies tells you quite clearly. The goals that most often rise to the top of the social studies list are:

- Knows United States history
- Knows United States geography
- Describes the structure and functions of local, state, and federal governments
- Knows laws governing citizens' behavior

Sound like 1920—U.S. history, U.S. geography, and U.S. civics? Those are old-fashioned, certainly. What comes next? World history and world geography usually come next—understandable in our age.

But what about anthropology, sociology, psychology, political science, social psychology, and even economics—those improvements added by the experts when they invented the "social studies"? They are there—but way down the list (though economics is gaining rapidly). Perhaps if those less important disciplines had not been added, social studies would still be as important as the other basic academic subjects. This is a case where "strengthening" the curriculum has evidently weakened it, a case where the experts have added so much social science ballast that history, geography, and civics are no longer enough helium to lift the balloon up among the top-ranking subjects where it used to be.

What emphasis are you placing on history, geography, and civics in your schools? What are your senior high school social studies electives focused on? Sociology and political science and psychology? Do you think 12:00 matters? The stakeholders do.

But Are These Your Results?

The purpose of these anecdotes—English and math, art and music, foreign languages, health, social studies— is *not* for you to act on these findings from our surveys in other districts. The purpose is to get you to think hard about these kinds of 12:00 issues and settle them for your own schools.

If you don't know what your own stakeholders would say on each issue, you probably should survey them to find out.

What To Do with the Results

Do you have to do exactly what your own survey results say? Of course not. You are elected or appointed to lead the schools at 12:00. What you do have to do is find out what the various stakeholders want, make sure you understand why they want it, and then let them know why you did or did not give them what they wanted.

Here is a case of one school board's *not* doing what the survey results said to do. Our survey for one large Midwestern city showed that foreign languages ranked at the bottom of the list of school subjects. In fact, the district was already about to close its foreign language program for lack of enrollment.

Upon seeing the survey results and realizing for the first time that everybody—school staff members included—thought foreign languages were unimportant, the school board members and top administrators decided to launch a massive public awareness campaign, along with a parallel professional awareness campaign. The focus of both campaigns was, of course, how important foreign languages really are. It was a two-year effort. By working very hard, that district doubled foreign language enrollment in those two short years. It was a spectacular case of *not* following public and professional opinion, but of using those opinions to understand how bad the problem really was—and to fix it. It was a spectacular case of school board leadership.

There is power in information. It makes you powerful to know that most of the public and most of the profession, for example, want "spectator" art and music, even though the parents of students in the band and choir are very vocal about "varsity" music. Yes, those vocal few will storm the door at your board meetings. But it makes you powerful to know that the people coming in the door are not speaking for everybody else—only for themselves. You, on the other hand, are elected or appointed to speak for everybody.

Does this mean that you should not have curriculum goals for the star performers—in art, music, physical education, and the rest? Of course not. That's why you have elective courses for those students.

What it does mean is that you must think very hard at 12:00 about the curriculum required for *all* of your students. Moreover, you should probably think about it *first*.

Selecting Objectives

If goals are the *broad* statements of what students can know, feel, or do, objectives are the *narrow* statements of what students can know, feel, or do. For example:

- *GOAL*: Knows world geography
- *OBJECTIVE*: Locates the continents on a map

In other words, the objective zeros in on one narrow piece of the broader goal. Objectives define the goal; they give the goal *one definition* out of *many possible definitions*. You can see that "Knows world geography" is an umbrella over many, many possible objectives that could be written.

Goals Cannot Be Learned; Only Objectives Can Be Learned. Until some or all of these possible objectives are written, there can be no learning. That is, children cannot learn broad goals; they can learn only narrow objectives. When they have learned the objectives, they have learned the goal—as defined by those particular objectives.

Goals Cannot Be Measured; Only Objectives Can Be Measured. Another equally important point is that goals cannot be measured; they cannot even be judged. A goal spans such a wide territory of possible objectives that, until that territory has been narrowed by selecting some of those objectives, a test (or a performance rating scale or some other means of measurement) cannot be put into place. Otherwise, a test might be placed in one logical part of the broad goal territory, while the children are being taught objectives in another equally logical, but different, part of the goal territory. In such a case, they would fail the test—even though they had learned something else equally important. Indeed, when test scores are unpleasantly low, the single most common complaint board members hear from professional educators is this:

"That test does not match our curriculum."

The test probably does match your goals; that is, it is probably located somewhere within the broad territory of your goals. It probably does not match your objectives;

that is, the objectives are located somewhere else within the broad territory of your goals, so that they do not match the test.

And so, if you do not have any objectives at 12:00, you cannot have meaningful measurement at 9:00.

Sample Objectives

In order to illustrate the 10,000 to 15,000 objectives you will need at 12:00, here are some examples taken from the four basic academic subjects. Notice their specificity (especially relative to the goals, cited earlier), their clarity, and their freedom from educational jargon, which would prevent lay people like board members from understanding them. The sample objectives are taken from the elementary school grades, the middle or junior high school grades, and the high school grades.

Elementary School

- Identifies by sight and sound short vowel sounds in a word: *a*, *e*, *i*, *o*, and *u*
- Associates cardinal numbers (1-10) and ordinal numbers (first-tenth)
- Infers reasonable conclusions from a reading selection
- Adds all combinations of one-digit, two-digit, and three-digit numbers (without carrying)
- Describes the life cycle of a butterfly
- Uses a globe to locate places (e.g., continents, countries)
- Uses guide words to locate words in a glossary or dictionary
- Checks the accuracy of answers to addition problems by re-adding and to subtraction problems by adding

- Diagrams a food chain
- Compares and contrasts the old and new life styles of the Navajo Indians
- Subtracts fractions with unlike denominators through 10
- Classifies rocks by their method of formation: igneous, metamorphic, and sedimentary
- Compares and contrasts the executive, legislative, and judicial branches of the state government
- Writes an editorial
- Applies the concept of molecular motion to solids, liquids, and gases
- Empathizes with the feelings of dilemma, loyalty, and patriotism Robert E. Lee felt towards the Union and the Confederacy

Middle/Junior High School

- Finds the area of squares and rectangles in customary and metric units of measure, using memorized formulas ($A = s^2$; $A = l \times w$)
- Knows the features of a tundra biome (e.g., frozen ground, short summers, long daylight hours)
- Knows the contributions of Homer, Sappho, Sophocles, Aesop, Socrates, and Hippocrates to philosophy and literature
- Writes paragraphs in which the tense is maintained consistently
- Finds the square root of any three-digit through five-digit number that is a perfect square greater than 225
- Appreciates the importance of following directions when handling science equipment (e.g., glassware, Bunsen burner)
- Compares and contrasts farming practices of industrialized and developing nations

- Gives a four-minute extemporaneous book review
- Conducts experiments to determine physical and chemical properties of matter
- Understands the Monroe Doctrine

High School

- Composes complex sentences with restrictive and nonrestrictive adjective clauses
- Uses absolute value in simplifying algebraic expressions
- Analyzes the cultural influences of the French and Spanish presence in North America
- Identifies the tone used by an author in a poem
- Divides polynomials by polynomials
- Analyzes the themes of a novel
- Determines whether two given lines are parallel, using the appropriate theorems and corollaries
- Analyzes acid-base reactions
- Explains the immediate and long-range effects of the French Revolution
- Solves quadratic equations, using the quadratic formula
- Explains how Newton's Second Law of Motion applies to a variety of situations (e.g., hitting a baseball, a falling rock, parachuting)
- Evaluates the impact of international defense and economic associations (e.g., NATO, SEATO, the Common Market, the Warsaw Pact)

That is what they sound like. Now, how many should there be? We already said 10,000 to 15,000, if you govern a K-12 district and have the usual array of electives in the high school, including vocational education courses. But, just to get a handle on a couple of grades in the elementary or middle/junior high school years, here are the numbers of objectives you might expect in *each* of the four basic academic subjects:

Grade	Objectives in *Each* Academic Subject
3	80
5	90
8	100

We find that English and math typically have slightly fewer objectives than these ballpark figures, and science and social studies have somewhat more objectives— regardless of the grade.

There is no magic number. That's what we tell teachers when we work with them directly to create the objectives. But, on the other hand, these approximations let you know to expect more that 25 per subject per grade —which is all some school districts have now. That's not enough for you to expect of students at 12:00.

How Do You Get 10,000 to 15,000 Objectives?

From where do you get the many objectives you will need to define your goals? There are several possibilities:

- *Get Them Automatically When You Buy Textbooks.* You can adopt objectives automatically (and perhaps unknowingly) when you buy a new set of textbooks.

Just as there can be no learning without objectives
and there can be no measurement without objectives,
there can be no textbooks without objectives. Textbooks cannot be written to match broad goals; all
textbooks are based on objectives chosen by the au-
thors.

- *Get Them from Your State Education Department.* In
  more and more states, the state education department
  itself publishes lists of objectives for various subjects
  in various grades. The state may send you these objectives as options for you to consider or as mandates
  for you to follow. Either way, they are likely to be a
  minimum set. You will definitely want to add others.

- *Have Your Teachers Write Them.* This is by far the
  most common method used by schools for developing objectives for their goals. You have probably already paid for many objectives to be written by your
  own teachers, serving on various curriculum committees, since you have been on the school board.

The third method, which we recommend, has its
own variations. Sometimes teachers write objectives out
of their heads, based on their own training and teaching
experience (remember the art, music, and foreign language cases). Sometimes teachers copy objectives straight
out of their textbooks (textbook publishers usually include them in the teachers' editions). Sometimes teachers
take them out of other teaching materials (films, film-
strips, reference books, or outside reading books) used
with students.

In fact, teachers should use *all* of these sources in
writing objectives—*plus* any objectives or curriculum
guidelines issued by your state education department,
any state tests your students take, any national tests your
students take, other good textbooks not currently used in
your school district, and so on. Having teachers use a
great variety of sources in writing the objectives is your

best insurance that your curriculum will include a comprehensive set of important learnings in each school subject.

How Many Teachers Will You Need? How many teachers will you need to write your objectives? That is more a matter of politics than anything else. The intellectual work of writing objectives can probably be done best by choosing the teacher most knowledgeable about a subject in a grade and having that teacher alone write the objectives for that subject in that grade—say, third grade science. Writing, as we all know, is a solitary—not a group—activity.

However, many times individual teachers tell us that they do not feel comfortable speaking for all of the other teachers in their grade for any subject, even though they may be very knowledgeable about that grade and that subject. Therefore, we recommend that two teachers from each grade be selected to write the objectives in each subject. That could be two teachers per subject for a total of as many as 20 teachers per grade (more in the high school) or, if your school district is small, it could be the same two or four or six or eight teachers doing all the subjects. In any case, two teachers working together on third grade science gives each teacher someone to bounce ideas off of and some confidence in the relatively scary task of speaking for many colleagues; yet, they can't slow each other down too much by wasting time in long meetings where no one is actually getting any writing done.

Two teachers per subject per grade (per course per grade, in most high schools) *cannot* buy you much acceptance of the objectives by the remaining teachers—unless you have a very small school district. But, we'll tell you how to get teachers' acceptance of the objectives a bit later in this chapter. You must do it; you just cannot do it during the initial writing of the objectives.

How Long Will It Take Them? How quickly do you want 12:00 done? How important is it to you to get things straightened out? The objectives can be written much faster than you or your administrators think. Here is the most typical story we hear when we start working in a school district:

> "We've had a teachers' committee rewriting our reading objectives for the past two years, and we're almost finished," the curriculum director will say.

Allowing objectives writing to take that long gives a bad message to your teachers: No one cares if you ever get this finished. It also deprives the teachers of the sense of accomplishment they would have gotten if they had finished the work more quickly, gotten it into the classrooms, and seen the fruits of their labors in increased student achievement.

It shouldn't take more than 30 to 40 hours of professional work for one or two teachers to produce a set of objectives for a subject in a grade—like third grade science. Those hours can be scheduled in one week (in the summer, for example), spread out over a month (on weekends and in the evenings, for example), spread out over a semester (by releasing teachers from classes, for example), or even over a full school year. It's still just 30 to 40 hours of professional working time.

We once worked in a small Minnesota school district unusually intent on getting the job done. The district produced new objectives for every subject in every grade K-12 in about four months. Much of the time was spent by our staff in New York editing the teachers' work and returning it to them with detailed comments to improve it. That whole process—iterations of writing and editing between the teachers and us—took only four months. The moral of the story is this: It doesn't have to take years, and you don't have to do only one subject at a time.

Why do most school districts do one subject (or maybe two) at a time? There are two simple reasons: (1) your central office administrators feel *they* are too busy to handle more (the *teachers* aren't too busy, inasmuch as most teachers probably won't be involved at all); and (2) your textbook adoption and purchase cycle may have enough money each year to replenish books in only one or two subjects. It's a shame to let the purchase of textbooks dictate how many subjects' objectives you can fix at one time. It's rather like the tail wagging the dog.

Remember: You may not do it in four months, but it need not take four years, either.

How Often Do You Need To Revise the Objectives? Most subjects do not undergo much change in *what* can be taught at the elementary and secondary school levels in even 10 years. Yes, some new history will happen, some new literature will be written, some new scientific discoveries will be made. Such new events can be added to your objectives easily, without calling into question the objectives already in place. In other words, some updating through important additions is fine—it can even be annual, if you want to keep on your toes as a district. But major revisions once you get 12:00 objectives carefully arranged? Probably not once every 10 years. Writing the objectives the first time will cost you some time, money, and anxiety, but the investment will last you for years.

What Are Board Members Supposed To Do about the Objectives Once They Are Written?

Of course, you will not be writing the 10,000 to 15,000 objectives needed to cover all the grades and all the subjects taught in your schools. But you must make sure that your teachers write them and give them to you. When you get them, you must read them and think very hard about them before you adopt them as school board property. If you have a stamp that says "Property of the Board of Education," the most important place to use that stamp is on your objectives.

At this point in the discussion, some school board members begin to squirm in their chairs. It is because they think that they do not know enough to establish 12:00 curriculum objectives—that they do not know enough even to read and review curriculum objectives written by professionals. We disagree.

Here are four lessons you can learn and use when you look at your district's objectives. Insisting that objectives meet certain simple standards will let you have a significant impact on improving the curriculum for your students.

1. Objectives Are Not Wallpaper; Objectives Are Guarantees.

Once we were reading a set of curriculum objectives from a good small school district way up North. We were particularly taken with the woodworking (senior high vocational education) and general music (kindergarten through sixth grade) objectives. As we read through the woodworking objectives, we were sure that the final objective was going to read: "Builds small cities." As we read through the general music objectives, it became crystal clear that Leonard Bernstein would have nothing on these sixth graders once they learned the objectives. They could conduct a symphony orchestra upon leaving elementary school. That's how ambitious the objectives were.

"How wonderful," you might think as a school board member. "Teachers should have high expectations."

"How terrible," we thought. "These are not expectations; these are pipe dreams."

We called in the woodworking and music teachers and had the following conversation:

> "You are not really teaching kids this much, are you?" we queried.
>
> "Of course not," the teachers answered. "We try, but most of them don't learn most of it."
>
> "Then why have you written all these objectives?" we continued.
>
> "Because the curriculum director asked us to. He is a nice guy. We go fishing with him in the summer, and we want to cooperate. He's had notebooks for the curriculum objectives printed with the district name. We wanted to fill up our section with important objectives. He likes them. What's the problem?" they asked.
>
> "The problem is that 9:00 is coming. Eventually your students will be tested on these objectives," we went on.
>
> "Tested?" they said with dismay.
>
> "Yes, tested. When it comes time for the school board to find out whether students are learning what is expected of them, the school board is going to ask you to produce test scores at 9:00 to show that the students have learned the 12:00 objectives," we explained as gently as we could.
>
> "Well then, we guess we have some revisions to do," they sighed.

This conversation is not unique. In fact, the problem is widespread. Most teachers believe—because you have let them believe it—that objectives are nothing but wallpaper decorating the offices of district administrators. They think no one will ever read them, much less use them, and they wonder why you keep paying teachers to write them.

Objectives must not be used as wallpaper. They must be used as guarantees of learning.

Professional educators do not view objectives as

guarantees. Both administrators and teachers view them as admirable—if unrealistic—aspirations. You must say to your administrators and you must get your administrators to say to your teachers, "Objectives are guarantees that you make to us for student learning. You must promise the board at 12:00 that students will learn them. And the board promises you that it will be waiting at 9:00 to make sure you kept your promise."

But, to take the teachers' side, we have to say again that you and your administrators have let them get the wrong idea for years. Once a group of 14 classroom teachers serving as curriculum committee chairpersons (one per school subject) said to us:

> "You know, no one will ever look at these objectives when we finish writing them. Not the school board. Not the central office administrators. Not even our principals. If the principals won't even read the objectives, they certainly won't supervise teachers to make sure they are being taught. So what's the point of having committees do all this work? This is just a waste of time."

"This can't be," we thought. We were sure that at least the principals—each of whom sat on one or more of the curriculum committees—would read the objectives. We were sure that the principals would study them and talk about them with teachers in their own schools. We were sure that the principals would watch when they went into the classrooms to see that the objectives were being taught. We were so sure that we said to the group of chairpersons:

> "Here's what we'll do. Each one of you make up a test on the objectives in your subject—a test for principals. Make it a test that the principals could pass *only* if they had read and studied your objectives. Now, don't write a test of science knowledge, but a test about the science *objectives*. For instance, you could ask: Where do we start teaching about energy? In what grades will we need laboratory time? Where are we going to hit the debate about evolution versus creationism?

"Then we will have the superintendent give two tests to the principals every month at their regular principals' meetings. We'll make the principals members in a subjects-of-the-month club, with tests at every club meeting. And, by the end of the school year, the principals will be experts in all the objectives for all the subjects."

The chairpersons were delighted. At last someone would be paying attention to what the curriculum committees had written. We were delighted. We thought it was a great way to make sure that the new objectives did not become just wallpaper. The superintendent and his assistants were less delighted. The principals were not delighted at all. In fact, after a heated debate in a principals' meeting and some private meetings with the superintendent, they refused to take the tests. That's when we realized the teachers were exactly right. The principals were not going to read the objectives. And they had the superintendent's sympathy: He was not going to read them, either.

Do you have principals like that? If you do, that's your superintendent's fault. Your superintendent hired them at 3:00. If your superintendent won't read the 12:00 objectives, that's your fault.

If you do not intend to make teachers and principals use the objectives you adopt, don't bother your teachers with writing them and don't bother the board with adopting them. Don't bother to think about the most important things you need to run the curriculum clock: the 12:00 objectives.

2. Objectives Must Not Be Repeated Verbatim from Grade to Grade.

If you can correct this one problem, it will do more to raise learning standards in your schools than any other single thing you can do. This problem occurs in many—

indeed, most—schools. Here is how it came to our attention.

We were reading through mathematics objectives from kindergarten through twelfth grade in one school district. In fourth grade, we noticed the objective: "Adds fractions." In fifth grade, we noticed the objective: "Adds fractions." In sixth grade, we noticed the objective: "Adds fractions." In seventh grade, we noticed the objective: "Adds fractions."

We called in the mathematics curriculum committee and asked why students were taught to add fractions over and over again for four years. One teacher explained:

> "Well, you know, some kids just never learn to add fractions. We try to teach it to them in fourth grade. But they don't all learn it. So we try again in fifth grade. Some still have trouble. So we try it again in sixth grade. A few more get it, but not all of them. So we try again in seventh grade, hoping to catch the rest."

Sound sensible to you? Not to us. We thought instead that it was pretty convenient. The fourth grade teachers could say to themselves, "Well, if half of the class doesn't learn to add fractions this year, my friends down the hall will take care of it next year in fifth grade." Then the fifth grade teachers could say to themselves, "Well, we tried. But some of the kids still don't have it. That doesn't matter. Our friends down the hall will take care of it in sixth grade next year." And so on.

With reasoning like this, no teachers ever had to be accountable for teaching the students to add fractions. If sixth grade teachers didn't teach it, they would pass the kids along the line to the next grade. After all, adding fractions was scheduled to be learned in seventh grade, too. That is a good design for a remedial program, but a bad design for a regular curriculum.

Rungs on a Learning Ladder. Classroom teachers never let themselves forget that some students do not learn what they should. That dismal fact—true in almost every classroom—makes some teachers stay after school, keeps others awake at night, and brings others back early in the morning. To their credit, the best teachers try and try again to bring up the hindmost. In fact, some people worry that such teachers lose the top half of the class while working with the bottom.

When good teachers like these sit on curriculum committees, they bring this mindset with them. Because they are accustomed to repeating and reviewing for slow students in their classes, they tend to rubber stamp the same objective into grade after grade, knowing some students will miss it. This is how we talk to curriculum committees:

> "Put the objective in the grade where you believe about 75 percent of the students can learn it—and remember it. Think of the 75 percent as the middle half (50 percent) of the class plus the top quarter (25 percent) of the class. Assume that if the typical teacher can teach the objective to the middle 50 percent, he or she can certainly teach it to the top 25 percent.

> "What we want you to do is schedule the objective to be learned in that grade because 75 percent of the students can learn it in that grade. We recognize fully that not all students will learn it on schedule. You can design remedial programs for them—and you should, but only after you finish designing the regular curriculum ladder for the regular students.

> "Do not repeat that objective in any later grade. Those later grades will have their own work to do. They won't have room to repeat objectives from earlier grades. That repetition will have to take place in remedial programs.

> "When you leave the curriculum committee and go back into your own classroom in September with the objectives assigned to your grade, you will undoubtedly find some students who have not learned all of last year's objectives. You may decide that you have to review last year's objectives with those stu-

dents before teaching this year's objectives. That's fine. But
both you and the students must understand that the review is
not new learning for your grade. It is nothing but a review of
last year's work—even if it takes the first six weeks of this year
to finish the review. They are still last year's objectives, not this
year's objectives. Remembering that will be a handy reminder
to you—and, we hope, to everyone else who is paying
attention—that you are having to convert the first six weeks of
your year into a remedial program. It will remind you to ask
the principal and other teachers whether there is not some better way to accomplish remediation than that."

Let's make it clear, however, that committees that
write ladders of objectives should be allowed to repeat
topics from year to year: topics such as paragraphs,
weather, colonization, or even fractions. But, each year,
they must add something different, new, more elaborate,
more difficult—a *more advanced* objective, which justi-
fies the topic's repetition. Take our fractions objective as
an example. "Adds fractions with like denominators less
than 12" might be placed in one grade, "Adds fractions
with like denominators of 12 or greater" might be placed
in a later grade, "Adds fractions with unlike denominators less than 12" in a still later grade, and so on. That
makes sense. Each succeeding objective on the same topic
is more advanced. That's what a *spiral curriculum* is all
about: The same topic is revisited in a later grade with
more challenging objectives.

What a spiral curriculum is *not* about is repeating
the same objectives, the same learning, year after year.
That's what some professional educators think it is. But
it's not. We prefer to call that a wheel-spinning curriculum. It is a plan for no progress. If American history ap-
pears in grades 5, 8, and 11, it had better be more
advanced every time it shows up again. Otherwise, it
would be boring to students and a waste of tax dollars as
well.

Just so you will know exactly what a wheel-spinning curriculum looks like, here are two sample pages of English objectives (pp. 82–83)—one from grades 4–8 and one from grades 9–12. These are actual examples taken from two different school districts. The X's show the grade in which each objective is to be learned. The objectives themselves are not very good (most real examples aren't), but we didn't edit them. See the wheel spin.

English teachers are notorious for producing lists of objectives like these examples. We once worked with teachers to design a reading curriculum for all grade 1–9 students in a big city. We adopted the "no repetition" rule. By the time teachers had finished the grade 6 objectives, they had used up all the objectives that had previously been taught in grades 7, 8, and 9. How did that happen? Well, there had been so much repetition of objectives in grades 1–6 that when the "no repetition" rule removed them, the remaining objectives were like loosely-packed cookies in a big cookie box. Shaking down those remaining objectives left so much empty space that the elementary teachers were forced to rob the junior high of their objectives in order to fill the elementary cookie box.

There are two points to this story: (1) repetition had made the elementary curriculum too loose; and (2) repetition had made the junior high curriculum nothing but a copy of the elementary curriculum. You might say that the entire grades 1–9 curriculum had been designed as a remedial program—designed for those students who would *fail* to learn the objectives rather than for those students who would *succeed* in learning them. It was a plan for no progress, designed for those students who were expected to make no progress. The effect of the plan was to doom all students to no progress.

Robbed of their former objectives, the junior high teachers had to create an entirely new, more advanced,

GRADES 4–8
ENGLISH OBJECTIVES

OBJECTIVE	GRADE IN WHICH OBJECTIVE IS TO BE LEARNED				
	4	5	6	7	8
Recalls story details and locates answers for questions in a selection or story	X	X	X	X	X
Understands the development of plot, including stages of development, climax, and plot resolution	X	X	X	X	X
Identifies the story setting	X	X	X	X	X
Recognizes the author's purpose for writing (inform, describe, or entertain)	X*	X	X	X	X
Recognizes problems and creates solutions	X	X	X	X	X
Identifies the meaning of unknown words or phrases by using picture clues or by using known words and phrases	X*	X	X	X	X
Recognizes the sequence of events by using cue words that signal occurrences within the story	X	X	X	X	X
Identifies the sequence of events when cue words are not stated	X	X	X	X	X
Recognizes that certain events precede and follow an event	X	X	X	X	X
Classifies and categorizes words, phrases, and ideas	X	X	X	X	X
Expresses an opinion about a given selection	X	X	X	X	X
Distinguishes between statements of fact and opinion	X	X	X	X	X
Identifies a selection as realism or fantasy	X*	X	X	X	X
Makes and defends an answer, judgment, or opinion	X*	X	X	X	X
Identifies cause and effect relationships	X	X	X	X	X
Draws conclusions and justifies them	X	X	X	X	X
Summarizes the information contained in a selection	X	X	X	X	X
Makes predictions about story outcomes	X*	X	X	X	X
Infers the theme of a selection	X	X	X	X	X

*This objective was also used in at least one grade below fourth grade.

GRADES 9-12
ENGLISH OBJECTIVES

OBJECTIVE	GRADE IN WHICH OBJECTIVE IS TO BE LEARNED			
	9	10	11	12
Recognizes and uses appositives	X	X	X	X
Recognizes and uses direct address	X	X	X	X
Recognizes and uses predicate nominatives	X	X	X	X
Recognizes and uses plural and possessive forms	X	X	X	X
Recognizes and uses predicate objects	X	X	X	X
Recognizes and uses adverbs and adverb phrases in sentences	X	X	X	X
Identifies and uses adverbial nouns, objective complements, and retained objects	X	X	X	X
Identifies and uses adjectives and adverbs	X	X	X	X
Recognizes and uses adjectives and adjective phrases in sentences	X	X	X	X
Knows and uses comparative and superlative forms of adjectives and adverbs	X	X	X	X
Identifies and uses conjunctions	X	X	X	X
Identifies and uses coordinating conjunctions	X	X	X	X
Identifies and uses subordinating conjunctions	X	X	X	X
Identifies and uses correlative conjunctions	X	X	X	X
Identifies and uses prepositions and prepositional phrases	X	X	X	X
Identifies interjections	X	X	X	X
Uses clues to identify the eight parts of speech	X	X	X	X
Knows and uses the rules of capitalization	X	X	X	X
Knows and uses the rules of punctuation	X	X	X	X
Uses periods when necessary	X	X	X	X
Uses commas correctly	X	X	X	X

more challenging set of objectives for grades 7, 8, and 9. In the end, the school district had a learning ladder in which every reading rung moved higher and higher.

The mistake of repeating objectives is not made just by teachers on local curriculum committees. It is made by textbook publishers as well. That's even worse, because it damages the curriculum in thousands of school districts nationwide.

We once looked at a set of writing textbooks for grades 9, 10, 11, and 12. They were quite attractive. They were even well written. There was only one problem. They were all alike. Only the covers were different.

Yes, some of the *exercises* and some of the *examples* changed from year to year, but each year students learned what a paragraph was, how a paragraph might be developed, how an essay should be structured, and how to prepare a research report. Students do not need to learn that four years in a row. That would be boring.

You must make sure that the objectives progress from year to year, even though not all students will keep perfect pace with that progression. The curriculum objectives your teachers write must be for the large majority of students—about 75 percent—and they must challenge those students each year by expecting more and more learning.

For those students—perhaps 25 percent (though, in our experience, it will turn out to be *far* fewer)—whose feet slip off the rungs of the learning stepladder, you will need to supply as much good remedial help as you can, just as you are doing now, we hope. But the fact that *some* students need remediation is no reason to avoid building a stepladder for the majority of students—a stepladder that progresses from rung to rung without repetition.

One last point some of you will hear from your teachers:

"We have a system here in our district where we *introduce* an objective in grade 3, *teach* it in grade 4, *expand* on it in grade 5, *elaborate* on it in grade 6, have students *master* it in grade 7, and *test* it in grade 8. That's the way we do it here."

Maybe we have exaggerated that quotation a little, but not much. You may hear something a lot like it, especially in reading. When we have worked in schools with that system, we have found that most teachers cannot tell you the difference between introducing an objective, expanding on it, elaborating on it, and so on. They do not know what *their* job is in contrast to the jobs of the teachers before and after them.

Most teachers would just as soon be told, "Teach this objective this year so that the students learn and remember it." That's a lot simpler. More important, it lets teachers in each grade know what is expected of them in that grade—and what they must expect of their students. The 12:00 objectives you expect your teachers in each grade to deliver must not be a mystery to them.

3. Objectives Are Not Ice Floes.

Your school district's objectives should be just that—your *district's*. That means they are the property of the district—not of the individual teachers, not of the high school science department, not of the individual schools. (Remember your 12:00 stamp: "Property of the Board of Education.")

In many school districts—we probably could say, in most school districts—objectives are like ice floes. They float, shifting continuously, moving with the undercurrents of changing teachers, changing courses, changing administrators, changing times. This is especially true in high schools, particularly in elective courses. The movement often goes unnoticed by the school board—unnoticed, unconsidered, and thus uncontrolled.

Here are several real examples that may sound all too familiar to you.

- *Goodbye, Creative Writing*

    "We're dropping creative writing," the high school principal explained to the superintendent.

    "Why?" she asked.

    "Because Diane Rusling is retiring. You remember, Diane started that course, and she made it what it was. But I don't have any other teachers who can teach it the way Diane does. The kids just wouldn't be excited. So, we're dropping it."

- *Farewell, Canada*

    "We're dropping Canada, Our Good Neighbor to the North," the high school principal said to the superintendent.

    "Why?" he asked.

    "Because Dave Court is transferring out of the district. You remember, Dave is Canadian. When he came to teach here, we added this elective. It's been very popular. But, of course, I don't have any other Canadian teachers. So, this is the last time this elective will be offered," the principal explained.

- *Hold Steady, Bees*

    "The science curriculum committee has recommended that seventh grade be devoted to life science, eighth grade to earth science, and ninth grade to physical science," explained the junior high school principal to the superintendent. "I have accepted that recommendation. However, one of my eighth grade teachers is a bees enthusiast. He keeps bees himself at home and does an extremely interesting unit on bees in eighth grade for about six weeks every year. The kids love it.

    "Now, I know that bees are not part of earth science and, therefore, don't really belong in the eighth grade.

However, because the eighth graders like the bees unit so much, I've decided to let it stay in that particular eighth grade teacher's curriculum. Of course, the other two eighth grade teachers won't be teaching the bees unit."

"Okay," said the superintendent. "No problem. I remember when my own kid had bees in eighth grade. He liked 'em."

• *Hello, Watercolors*

"I have my objectives right here," the high school art department chairperson said to the superintendent. "They're for ceramics, oils, and charcoal drawing. That's what I teach in the Art IV course. I brought these objectives with me when I came to the district, and I'll be taking them away with me when I go. I don't know how much you know about the way art teachers work, but these objectives are nothing like the ones I found when I came to the high school three years ago. And it would be a professional insult for me to leave these objectives behind for the next art teacher. She'll have her own specialties, just as I do. Suppose the new person has no training in oils and wants to do watercolors instead? She'll do watercolors."

Sound familiar? Does your district's curriculum come and go with your teachers? Does the fact that teachers retire or move or transfer have a dramatic effect on your curriculum? Does the fact that teachers have personal interests—unrelated to the curriculum—reshape your curriculum?

Suppose you had been there on the four occasions described above? What would you have said? What would you have said when the superintendent brought those curriculum recommendations to the board table for a vote? Maybe you don't even know when objectives—or even whole courses—are being dropped or added. You should: 12:00 is your territory.

Here are some things you might have said—some things you *should* have said.

- "Ms. Superintendent, you'd better arrange for another high school English teacher to get some training in creative writing. We feel creative writing is an important part of the high school English elective program, and we can't have it dropped because Diane retires."

- "Mr. Superintendent, you'd better get Dave to hand over his notes to another high school social studies teacher. Perhaps Dave should spend some time with that teacher to explain more about Canada and to discuss whatever the other teacher doesn't understand. Maybe that other teacher should take a college course on Canada. After all, we're located very close to Canada, and we feel it is an important part of our social studies curriculum. The board needs better reasons to change the curriculum than the ones you're giving us.

  "Besides, if we happen to hire someone named Manuel Juarez to fill Dave's spot, are you going to recommend we have a course called Mexico, Our Good Neighbor to the South?"

- "Ms. Superintendent, we don't believe we can allow one teacher's six-week unit on bees to interrupt a 36-week course on earth science for eighth graders. Those eighth graders would miss six weeks of earth science that the other eighth graders would be getting. Why don't you let the beekeeper start an after-school club about keeping bees? We're sure it will be real popular."

- "Mr. Superintendent, remind your art teacher that the 12:00 objectives are the property of the board of education. He's in our territory now, and we want steady objectives. Maybe he'd like to teach in the next county?"

Yes, school board members can—and do—say things like that. Yes, you do know enough.

4. Objectives for Required versus Elective Courses Must Be Carefully Sorted Out.

Here's a problem that came directly to the board table in one school district. Maybe you have had a similar problem. A mother stood up during the public participation section of the board meeting and challenged the school board and superintendent with the following story:

> "Last week I was looking over an essay on a college application my twelfth grade daughter, Charlotte, had written. I thought it was pretty bad—too bad to send to a college.
>
> "I asked Charlotte whether she wrote like this in her classes. She said that she guessed she did. I asked her how her English teachers put up with this and why they weren't more demanding.
>
> "She recalled for me the string of high school elective English courses she'd taken, starting in the tenth grade: Sports Literature, Public Speaking, Reading Improvement, Film Study, Dramatics, and Views of Minorities. Charlotte told me not much writing had been required in any of those courses. I was dismayed.
>
> "I come to you tonight to ask how you can be graduating students from high school when they cannot write. I further ask how you can be graduating students from high school when you have not even tried to teach them to write. This is unacceptable to me as a parent and as a taxpayer and as an employer in this town."

Have you designed your elective English courses—or let the professionals design your elective courses—in such a way that this question could ever come to you? If you have, the question might be coming any day now. Electives, as you know, were very popular in the late 1960s and in the 1970s. They were a way to make the curriculum "relevant" to your students. Maybe they did. Maybe they didn't.

But as the 1980s rolled around, electives became less

fashionable—perhaps because of questions like the one raised by Charlotte's mother. School districts started retreating from electives and started looking for firmer ground to build a curriculum on.

It's not just the parents who are upset. It's the colleges as well. We heard one story from the English chairperson in an excellent Illinois school district. She explained that college admissions committees were having trouble reading the transcripts her high school sent for students applying to college. The committees, it seems, could not make heads or tails of the computer-abbreviated English course titles. Imagine a college admissions officer's puzzlement at reading this tenth grade English course selection: "DEM AND DET." Now the high school English chairperson knew that meant "Demons and Detectives," but she was becoming uncertain whether even the full title would reassure the college admissions committees. One college finally said to her:

> "You will have to explain the content of your English courses to us. The titles won't do. And, by the way, if writing is not a part of the course, we will not consider it to be English."

How do you stabilize objectives in a high school subject like English? There are many ways. Perhaps you are already using some of them. One way, of course, is to go back to the old days of English I, English II, English III, and English IV: all required; no electives; no variation. Some districts have done just that—and with good success.

Here's another way. An English curriculum committee of teachers can determine a *required core* of objectives to be taught in each grade: a core for grade 9, a core for grade 10, a core for grade 11, and a core for grade 12. The core can be from the four basic English language skills: reading, writing, speaking, and listening. Then the required core of objectives for any grade can simply be adopted as the *backbone* of every elective course taught in that grade. Once every elective course has a backbone, other objectives particular to each elective can be added. For example, two different elective courses, say Twentieth Century American Fiction and English Poetry—both taught in grade 12—would have the identical core of reading, writing, speaking, and listening objectives. But each course would also have *additional* objectives of its own. So, no mother could come to the school board and say, "How can you graduate students from your high school if you have let them hopscotch through the curriculum, managing to avoid essential skills like writing for four years?"

Two Final Notes: An Inside Review of Your Objectives and an Outside Review of Your Objectives

The Inside Review. We promised to tell you how to get acceptance of the objectives by the teachers who did not write them. Getting teachers to accept the newly-written objectives is critically important for two reasons: (1) you want to make sure the teachers are willing to teach the new objectives; and (2) if 9:00 evidence of learning is not satisfactory, you don't want the teachers to blame the 12:00 objectives.

The best way to make sure that every teacher's voice is heard *before* you adopt the 12:00 objectives is to have your superintendent send a written survey to every teacher and to have your principals get a completed survey back from every teacher.

The survey is simple. It is a list of the new objectives, with several questions about each objective. Every teacher looks carefully at each separate objective, answers the questions about each one, and writes notes about objectives that should be added, changed, or eliminated.

Here are the questions we asked teachers in a survey in one school district—along with their answers:

Questions for Each Objective	Combined Answers for All Objectives
1. Is this objective *important* to teach in your grade?	86% YES
2. Do you know the *methods* for teaching this objective?	87% YES
3. Do you have the *materials* you need to teach this objective?	68% YES
4. Did you teach this objective to your students *last year*?	67% YES
5. Can you teach this objective to *90 percent* of your students next year?	50% YES

How would you interpret these results? It looks as if almost all teachers think the objectives written by the committees of their colleagues are important to teach and think they know how to do it; most teachers have the materials and taught the objectives last year; but only half think they can do the job with almost all of their students next year. They'll try, but they won't promise to succeed. We have seen better results in other districts with other circumstances; every case is different.

Have the superintendent send the results back to the objectives writing committees to guide a final editing of the objectives. Then have the superintendent forward the objectives, along with the survey results, to the board for review and official approval.

The Outside Review. We once worked with an outstanding school board in a suburban district of very bright students. The board members said to us, "Look, we're smart enough and we're educated enough to read and study and comment on all the objectives the superintendent brings in. But we just don't have the time it takes to do it. Where can we turn for help? We want somebody qualified—and independent of our own staff."

Together with the board, we came up with a list of "outside" reviewers—people beyond the school district boundaries—who could critique the district's objectives according to the very high standards the board had set when the objectives were created. The superintendent was instructed to have each set of objectives (for each course in each grade in each subject) reviewed by representatives of *several* of these groups:

- Nationally recognized experts in the subject field
- Professors in the subject field at selective colleges and universities (the kind their students attended)
- Faculty members in the subject field in comparable school districts
- Employers in the kinds of occupations for which a course prepares students (where applicable)
- Nationally recognized experts in the writing and use of objectives

We offered to put subject specialists in the state education department on the list, but the board members declined. They said their district was so much better than the state that state standards would be too low.

The board members agreed that they could review these outside critiques as a shortcut to reviewing the objectives. Then they could spend their time studying only those objectives that the critiques showed were in trouble.

Using outside reviewers accomplishes another purpose as well—even more important than saving board members' time. It guarantees that someone who knows more about the *subject* than your own teachers has a chance to catch any mistakes your teachers might have made in writing the objectives. You would be surprised at the number of mistakes teachers make in the actual *content* of their subjects. We could tell you about the social studies teacher in a top-notch suburban district in a Rocky Mountain state who wrote an objective about the contributions of nineteenth century American women, such as Florence Nightingale (Florence happened to be English). Such content mistakes are harder for board members to find than the kinds of problems we talked about earlier in this chapter—like unnecessary repetition of objectives. But someone has to catch them. Only qualified outsiders can do that for you.

We have developed a service in response to board members who want an outside appraisal of how good their objectives are. You could have this done by an organization like ours, or by an outstanding professor at a university, or by someone else you trust outside of your district. If you already have some objectives in place—as many districts do—starting with this kind of outside critique will show you how much work has to be done at 12:00 before you can run your curriculum clock with your current objectives.

When we are brought in to critique the objectives in any subject from kindergarten through grade 12, we judge the objectives on these five important characteristics:

- *Challenge*—Are the objectives challenging enough for students at each grade level? Are they numerous enough? Do they set high enough expectations? Do they build in difficulty from one grade to the next at a sufficient pace?

- *Importance*—Do the objectives contain the most important elements of the subject? Are some trivial?

- *Balance*—Are the objectives balanced with respect to cognitive, affective, and psychomotor learning—that is, thinking, feeling, and doing?

- *Specificity*—Are the objectives detailed enough? Are they specific enough to guide a new teacher? Are they specific enough to help choose teaching materials, such as textbooks? Are they specific enough to guide test question writing?

- *Clarity*—Are the objectives clearly stated? Are they easily understandable to educators and civilians? Do they avoid educational jargon? Are they written in correct English (proper grammar, usage, etc.)?

In addition to the assessment of the objectives on these five characteristics, we also supply an edited version of the objectives that gives detailed comments on individual objectives that need to be improved (e.g., wording changes, notations that objectives were repeated from earlier grades or were duplicated within the same grade, and indications of missing topics to be included). This nitty-gritty editing is most helpful to teachers' committees created to refine the objectives once board members have studied such a critique and decided how the objectives should be changed.

Remember, 12:00 is your territory. Take charge. Stamp the goals and objectives:

PROPERTY OF
THE BOARD OF EDUCATION

Preview: Getting Teachers To Use the Objectives

As we start moving the clock hands into professional territory, some board members understandably get a little worried that the objectives won't really get into the classrooms—that teachers won't really *use* them as the basis for their daily lessons.

Here is one thing you can do right before you hand the stamped objectives over the fence to your professional staff. Ask teachers on your writing committees to divide the objectives into marking periods for you—six weeks, nine weeks, or whatever you have in your school district.

This will have several benefits: (1) it will help teachers pace themselves in getting all the objectives taught during the year; (2) it will allow your administrators to know approximately where the teachers should be at any point in the year; (3) it will allow parents to know approximately where their children should be at any point in the year; and (4) it will allow you to give 9:00 tests at the end of each marking period if you decide you want some evidence of learning (or nonlearning) before the end of the year—when it's too late for anyone to do anything about it (more on this topic in the 9:00 chapter).

Teachers will still have flexibility *within* each marking period to schedule the objectives as they see fit. That is enough latitude for most teachers.

By the way, the idea of dividing the objectives into marking periods came to us from the teachers on a writing committee in a Georgia school district. Those teachers said:

> "We've raised our expectations of students so much during this curriculum revision that we're afraid our teachers won't be able to pace themselves well enough to get all of the objectives covered by May 31. Let's divide the objectives into marking periods to give our colleagues a hand."

The idea has worked very well in other school districts where we've worked since. The credit goes entirely to those Georgians.

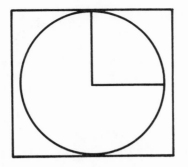

3:00   Selecting
Programs

Now we come to the superintendent's territory: deciding *how* to teach. When you cross the border, you enter the native land of the professional. That makes you a tourist in a foreign country. There are two things you *can* do: (1) you can observe the local customs; and (2) you can ask the natives to explain their ways. But there are two things you *cannot* do: (1) you cannot become a native; and (2) you cannot expect the natives to welcome your advice. Try to give too much advice and those initial professional smiles will evaporate; the summer air that greeted your arrival will become wintry. Teachers will react to your teaching suggestions the way your lawyer reacts to your legal suggestions. They will listen, probably politely, but they will pay no serious attention. Make too many suggestions and they will suggest, like your lawyer, that you had best leave the matter to them.

You cannot decide how the teachers should teach. You cannot even influence the decision very much. That is why setting goals and objectives at 12:00 and evaluating learning at 9:00 are so important for a board. When it comes to curriculum, that is the only kind of control you can get. You must control learning because you cannot control teaching.

Let's take a visit to the superintendent's territory starting at 3:00, not with the thought that you can control it, but with the thought that you ought to understand how the superintendent should control it. This chapter is called "Selecting Programs." What is a program?

As we said in "A Curriculum Clock," a program is some combination of these elements, listed here in order of importance:

1. Teachers
2. Parents
3. Times
4. Materials
5. Methods
6. Places

There are many alternatives for each separate element, and there are many, many possible combinations of elements—so many that it takes a skillful superintendent to know them all.

A civilian cannot know all the chemicals and all the combinations of chemicals for compounding a drug; only a trained pharmacist can. Moreover, what a civilian wants is an effect, an outcome, a result—to get well, not to compound the drug. A school board should stay on the outside of the druggist's counter, judging the treatment by its effect, not by its ingredients. It should judge the program at 9:00 by its effect on learning, not at 3:00 by the elements the superintendent compounds into it. To change an old phrase, the proof of the pudding is not in its recipe. Or, to go back to your lawyer, it is not how the case is prepared at 3:00 (or presented at 6:00) that should matter to you, but what the jury decides at 9:00. The board acts as jury, not as attorney; you do not prepare cases, you do not present cases—you decide on the evidence.

Think about what the superintendent has to consider at 3:00—as druggist, as attorney, as cook, as professional. Consider the possibilities.

1. Teachers

Many different kinds of people could be hired to teach. Teachers differ in amount, kind, place, quality, and recency of their own education. They differ in amount, kind, place, quality, and recency of their teaching experience. They differ in age, place of birth, appearance, sex, and life experience. They differ in intelligence and personality. They differ in interest in teaching, interest in their subject, and interest in students. They differ in classroom techniques, in whether they give homework and grade it, in whether they stop work at midafternoon or at midnight. They differ in what they cost on the payroll. The only thing they have in common is a teaching license. In everything else, they differ.

Nothing is more important at 3:00 than who teaches. No other element in the instructional program has as much influence on whether students learn as who their teachers are. Even so, school boards cannot pick teachers. They can only endorse the ones the superintendent brings in—or reject them and ask for more nominations, which does not guarantee that the new nominations will be any better. So, for practical purposes, the superintendent and the professional staff pick the teachers.

Over a number of years, the superintendent and the professional staff determine the overall composition of the teaching faculty: the balance (or imbalance) of young and old, energetic and lazy, inspiring and expiring, those who love the arts and those who love the sciences, those who love students and those who love summers.

That is just as it should be. You as a board member do not know enough to choose teachers; you cannot judge their potential at 3:00. But that is all right. You can judge their achievements at 9:00. And that is far more important.

2. Parents

Parents differ as much as teachers. They differ in education, occupation, income, life experience, ambition, interests, intelligence, personality, and energy. They differ in whether they see themselves as winners or losers, as people who control circumstances or are controlled by circumstances, as people who govern or are governed. They differ in whether they read or travel, in what they think about and what they talk about. They differ in the way they raise their children: whether they are home with their children or away at work, wheth er they talk with their children and what about, what they expect of their children in school and what they expect of them in life. They even differ in whether they live with their children or ever see them. The only thing they have in common is that they are parents. In everything else, they differ.

Next to who does the teaching, nothing is as important at 3:00 as who does the parenting. Nothing else influences learning as much. Parental background is a better predictor of what a child will do in school than a child's intelligence. This is probably because parents are the strongest influence on whether their children will apply their intelligence to their schooling, whether their children's actual school achievement will measure up to their potential school achievement.

Perhaps unfortunately, neither school boards nor superintendents get to pick the parents of their students. Headmasters of private schools may have that privilege, but officials in public schools do not.

Do you believe that parents are this important? Do parents themselves believe it? You may wonder about that when you hear the superintendent tell you how the students' homes are falling apart, forcing the schools into becoming virtual orphanages.

We once asked parents in a school district how important they were: "What percent of the credit do you deserve if your children learn the basic skills in school? What percent of the blame do you deserve if they don't?" (We thought we could average the two figures and come up with a fair answer.)

They gave us a range of answers:

"10%."

"90%."

"None."

"50%."

"5%."

"All."

"Depends on which parents."

"30%."

"40%."

"25%."

On the average, they took about 30 percent of the blame —or credit. We thought that was a lot—maybe too much.

So we began asking professional educators, thinking they would have a more realistic view of parents. In fact, we asked *professional educators who are parents,* because they walk on both sides of the street. We said, "Being realistic, what percent of the credit or blame would you take as parents in your own home, with your own children?"

The percent was not 30—not from these people who knew best what the home could accomplish versus what the schools could accomplish. It was 50. These professionals gave themselves half the credit as parents and the other half to teachers.

So if you ever want to know just how important parents are, ask them. And if you really want to know, ask professionals who are parents.

Researchers have not been able to establish whether it is what parents *are* (their background and personal characteristics) or what parents *do* (their specific child-rearing practices) that is more important in shaping how much their children learn in school. Common sense and personal observation tell us that it is some of each. Children are shaped both by what their parents are like and by what their parents do.

The topic is important because, while school officials cannot get all parents to *be* like the best parents, they might get more parents to *act* like the best parents so as to improve learning. That is, since parents are such an important element in an instructional program, school officials would be wise to spend time and money getting that element to work right. A superintendent who knows what parents should do and knows how to get them to do it should spend more time and effort on that element of the program than on some less important element—such as classroom teaching techniques. Whether the parents acted right—based on your superintendent's advice to them—will become clear at 9:00.

3. Times

Researchers have come up with something every one of you already knew: The longer students spend studying something, the better they learn it. Next to who does the teaching and who does the parenting, the amount of time scheduled for teaching (and for study) is most powerful in determining how much students will learn. That is one reason most state education departments stipulate minimum times for elementary school subjects and one reason the "Carnegie units" required for graduation are units of time spent in high school subjects.

To demonstrate how important time is, we can take the much-discussed business of "remedial" instruction for students who did not learn something the first time around. After hundreds of years of experience and decades of research, the education profession still has only one firm idea about remediation: The student must spend more time. That extra time can be before school or after school or in the evenings or on weekends or in the summers; but, unless the remedial student spends more time, the student will not learn the material or get the skills. For remedial instruction, the place does not seem to matter, or the method, or the materials, or even who teaches—another student, a tutor, a parent, or even a teacher. But the time does. Indeed, the very term "slow learner" simultaneously describes the problem and prescribes the solution.

Time spent is a significant element in the instructional program for all students, of course, not only for the slow. But you as a board member, you do not know enough to build a school schedule. Only the superintendent knows how much time to allocate to kindergarten music, third grade science, eighth grade mathematics, or eleventh grade physical education at 3:00 to produce the learning you have called for at 12:00. One reason is that the superintendent has to factor in all the other program elements while building a schedule: who will be teaching and where and how and with what materials and with what help from parents.

Whether the superintendent scheduled instruction correctly will, of course, not become clear until the clock hands reach 9:00.

4. Materials

Using the term "materials" broadly, there are many different kinds of materials and equipment available for instructing students. They include textbooks, maps, globes, workbooks, reference books, library books, films, drawings, photographs, models, recordings, clay, paint, construction paper, lumber, microscopes, chemicals, plants, animals, welding torches, tubas, automobiles, thread, ink, basketballs, French curves, flour, seesaws, refrigerators, test tubes, duplicating machines, poster boards, band saws, dolls, blocks, wrestling mats, brake shoes, towels, eggs, kilns, word processors, computers, and so on almost without end.

It takes trained professionals to know what to buy for kindergarten rooms, industrial arts shops, art rooms, chemistry labs, gymnasiums, football fields, music rooms, biology labs, home economics rooms, third grade classrooms, special education rooms, tenth grade classrooms, and all of the others. It is a question of not only what to buy, but also how much, which brands, and at what prices. And it is a matter of deciding when to replace existing materials. Will the typewriters last one more year? Can the science textbooks go another season? Should we replace the trombones or the trampolines?

Board members cannot make such decisions. Only the superintendent and the professional staff can do that. Moreover, whether they are buying the right things cannot be decided by logical analysis or good judgment alone at 3:00. No one—not you, not the professional staff—will know until the evidence of learning is gathered, analyzed, and summarized at 9:00. Thus, you should leave the choice of materials to the professionals and wait for the evidence to roll in when the clock hands reach 9:00. Of course, you will have to insist that the evidence of learning be presented to you for careful examination at 9:00. The only way the board can leave the 3:00 choice of materials to the professionals with confidence is to meet the professionals at 9:00 and require the proof of learning.

Among all the instructional materials, the textbook continues to be the most important by far. The reasons for this are discussed a bit later.

5. Methods

There are many methods of teaching. A reminder about what teaching and learning actually are might be helpful here.

- *To learn* is to do something you have never done be-fore—and to remember it so that you can do it again. The new learning can be a thought, a feeling, a move-ment, or some combination. But it has to be some-thing you have not known or understood before, or something you have not felt or believed before, or a way you have not moved your ams or legs or hands or feet before. Otherwise, you will not learn. By defini-tion, then, to learn is to do something new. And by definition, if you cannot remember it, you have not learned it.

  You may think that the second requirement is too strict—that students ought to be given credit for something they cannot remember (do not know now, do not feel now, and cannot do now) because they could do it at some time in the past. (If so, you will find yourself agreeing with some professionals.) But a little reflection on the practical applications of the second requirement will demonstrate that it is essen-tial. Otherwise, the schools would be full of students demanding credit for what they had forgotten, and the society would be full of people insisting on keep-ing jobs because they could do them in the past, even though they cannot do them now. By definition, then, if you don't remember it, you have, for practical purposes, not learned it.

- *To teach* is to get students to do things they have never done before and to remember them. Teachers somehow have to stimulate new behavior, then some-how cement it into place.

Teaching is not simply planning a series of lessons; a textbook could do that. Teaching is not simply presenting information; a film could do that. Teaching is not simply keeping order in the classroom; a guard could do that. Teaching is not simply assigning homework; a computer could do that. Teaching is not simply grading papers; a clerk or even a scoring machine could do that.

Teaching is not doing something; it is getting students to do something. Students do not learn what teachers do; students learn what students do.

The sentence "I taught it to them, but they did not learn it" is the ultimate *non sequitur* in the teaching profession. It ranks with "The operation was a success, but the patient died." Nonsense. If they did not learn it, the teacher did not teach it. By definition, to teach is to produce learning. And that is why teaching methods cannot be judged at 3:00. They cannot be judged until 9:00.

The reason that there are so many methods of teaching is that there are so many ways of getting people to try new things and so many ways of getting people to remember them.

Information—facts, formulas, definitions, theories —can be presented by lecture, oral reading by the teacher, films, recordings, television, radio, computer, posters, slides, transparencies, silent reading by the student, textbook study, demonstration by the teacher, blackboard notes, and in many other ways. Feelings, attitudes, values, and beliefs can be stimulated through the same means and by such others as discussion, trips, and projects. Movement can be stimulated through many of these means.

Once the students exhibit the desired thinking, feeling, or moving, there are many methods for getting them to remember it. The strategy is to get the students to *re-*

peat the behavior—*frequently* when they are first learning it so as to eliminate error, develop skill, and increase speed; *periodically* thereafter so that the new behavior does not fade with time. Because error can creep in, the behavior has to be watched and corrected while it is being repeated. Therefore, the strategy for producing memory is *guided practice over time.* (Not enough guidance, not enough practice, and not enough time is the formula for forgetting.) That is the strategy; there are many teaching tactics for carrying it out.

What method of teaching is best? No one knows. Probably none is "best." Teachers have debated the question for centuries, and researchers have probed it for decades. And both groups are still doing so today. But neither group has reached a conclusion—and probably never will.

For example, the most-debated, most-researched question is as unsettled today as ever: how to teach reading to beginners. As always, children are learning to read through many different methods: phonics and whole words, basal readers and computers, workbooks and library books—and, of course, whatever their parents come up with around the house, which has some children reading by the time they arrive at kindergarten.

Rather than one method's being best, it seems that many methods are best. According to one editorial:

> "Try to get a roomful of experts to agree on how best to teach reading. They can't. And what works best in mathematics: problem solving and estimation, or the rote work that so many teachers still assign? Reading and math are rock-bottom basics —yet there's still dissension." (*Phi Delta Kappan*, June 1987)

Teachers who have the greatest success use many methods. When one does not work, they use another, and then another until the student learns. A repertoire of methods lets the teacher handle any class, any student, any topic. Thus, the best teachers are not doctrinaire about methods. Keeping their eyes on 9:00, they try one thing after another at 3:00 until they get the learning they want at 9:00.

And, of course, that's what superintendents should do: keep their eyes on 9:00 and use any methods at 3:00 that will get the results they want.

You as a board member cannot choose the methods teachers will use in their classrooms. You should leave that to the professionals. But you should keep your eyes on 9:00—as always—to make sure the professionals chose right.

6. Places

There are not as many places as there are methods and materials, but there are nevertheless many places that could be chosen as sites for teaching. Some kinds of teaching can be conducted best in one, some in another. Some things can be learned best in a classroom, some at home, some in an office, some in a museum, some on a field trip to a pond.

Building, renovating, renting, or selecting places for learning, furnishing and equipping those places, and scheduling teachers and students into them is a job for a trained professional.

Board members can contribute little or nothing to the wise choice of location for learning, yet you probably spend more time on school buildings than on any other element of the instructional program. Presumably because it is so far removed from the central, influential elements of instruction and presumably because some board members have experience with construction or property management, you feel comfortable in dealing with the topic. That time is poorly spent, especially if it comes at the expense of your attention to 12:00 and 9:00—which it virtually always does.

How much does it matter where teaching takes place? It is probably the least important element in the instructional program. Given a good teacher, strong parental support for learning, sufficient time to teach, proper materials, and a variety of methods at the teacher's command, learning is likely to occur irrespective of the place. Conversely, even a great place cannot possibly make up for a poor teacher, indifferent parents, too little time, bad materials, and rigid adherence to one method of teaching.

That is why President James Garfield told the Williams College alumni back in 1871:

> "I am not willing that this discussion should close without mention of the value of a true teacher. Give me a log hut, with only a simple bench, Mark Hopkins on one end and I on the other, and you may have all the buildings, apparatus, and libraries without him."

Hopkins was a teacher so great that he made the place not matter. That is why Garfield would let the simple bench be put anywhere—so long as Hopkins came with it.

Admittedly, ordinary teachers cannot overcome ordinary places as well as Hopkins could. They need their libraries and laboratories and gymnasiums and shops and studios and wrestling rooms. Some things cannot be taught outside a biology laboratory or a printing shop or a soccer field or a ceramics room. It takes a professional to know what those things are—and what things can be taught as well in a lecture hall.

You as a board member cannot tell whether the place is right by poring over a blueprint of it at 3:00. You can tell only by waiting until 9:00 when the evidence of learning is turned in.

More about Textbooks

Let's return to the leftover matter of textbooks. Why are they the most important of all teaching materials? There are three reasons:

1. Textbooks have long been the substitute for the 12:00 goals and objectives. They are not a good substitute, partly because superintendents and board members treat textbook adoption as a 3:00 decision—a choice of teaching *materials*, which both parties correctly believe should be left to the professionals. Thus, textbook adoption customarily consists of a recommendation by the professional staff followed by a rubber stamp ceremony of endorsement by the board.

    Neither the board nor the professionals recognize that they are not determining *how* to teach as much as they are determining *what* to teach. If either group did, the conversation at textbook adoption time would be about the goals and objectives in the textbooks rather than about their other characteristics. The superintendent's recommendation would be backed up not only by rating sheets filled out by teacher's committees showing how good each textbook is as a teaching device, but also by analysis sheets showing what goals and objectives each textbook contains. The superintendent's recommendation would point to the textbook containing the most important things for students to learn—the things your board already picked at 12:00.

2. The second reason textbooks are the most important of all teaching materials is that some teachers do not know any more about their subject than the text-

books do. The textbooks are their only maps in a foreign land; they must follow their textbooks or get lost. There is good reason for the time-honored phrase, "Keep one chapter ahead of the kids." Such teachers need the textbook every bit as much as the students need it.

3. The third reason textbooks are important is that they embody the 3:00 teaching methods as well as the 12:00 goals and objectives and even the 9:00 measures of learning. Textbooks divide the information into bite-sized pieces, sequence it, schedule it, present it, and test it. What more could a teacher ask? No wonder textbook-centered teaching has withstood 50 years of relentless attack by professional leaders who have condemned it as unimaginative and boring. The textbook is a brilliant invention—quite possibly a necessity for a society dedicated to universal education, but unable to put a highly-qualified teacher in every one of its two million classrooms.

Textbooks would lose much of their importance to school boards—and, incidentally, to state legislatures—if school boards got real control over the 12:00 goals and objectives. If you did that, textbooks would be just teaching materials, rather than curriculum containers. Textbooks would then stipulate *how* to teach, but not *what*. Indeed, if your board controlled 12:00 as it should, the choice of textbooks could be left entirely to the professional staff. Whether the staff had chosen good textbooks would become clear, as always, at 9:00.

A school board in Colorado thought its way through textbook adoption recently. It entered the issue on one side, followed a consistent line of reasoning, and was surprised when it came out on the other side.

The superintendent's staff and the board began by embarking on a project to bring the 12:00 goals and objectives and the 9:00 measurement of learning under control. Once that was under way, they turned to the matter of textbooks, intending to stamp out the chaotic diversity in district textbooks by adopting a new policy requiring districtwide uniformity.

But some careful thought by the superintendent's staff led to this unexpected conclusion: The board can accomplish all the uniformity of learning it wants by bringing order to 12:00 and 9:00. That conclusion set off a surprising chain of reasoning. Since textbooks will no longer be used to control consistency of curriculum, there will no longer be any need for consistency of textbooks. Indeed, since textbooks have become 3:00 teaching devices rather than 12:00 curriculum containers and since a repertoire of teaching techniques is the best method of teaching, variety in textbooks should be encouraged rather than restricted. Therefore, textbook adoption should be decentralized to the school level—or even to the classroom teacher level—rather than controlled districtwide by the superintendent or by the board.

And so, to everyone's surprise, that became the official policy of the school board.

The moral of this story is that if you do your job at 12:00 and 9:00, you can free rather than control the professional staff at 3:00 and 6:00. You can get genuine control over something you can understand and actually care about—learning—rather than something you cannot understand and do not actually care about—teaching.

What the Board Can Do at 3:00— Well, at 2:45

The board's greatest single concern at 3:00 should be to make absolutely certain that everybody who designs programs at 3:00 gets told what those programs are designed to accomplish. What they are designed to accomplish is, of course, your 12:00 objectives. It is reasonable for you to insist that there be no confusion about this in the mind of anyone who makes decisions at 3:00.

Would such insistence bring the board across the boundary line, invading the professional staff's 3:00 territory? No, because you would stop short of saying *how* the objectives should be taught. You would simply say that all those who design programs must have a clear, official, easy-to-use copy of them. The board moves to 2:45, stops, and hands the objectives over the fence to the professionals. The board does not go over the fence, but the objectives do. That image is consistent with a central idea of the clock: The board does not determine how teachers should teach; the objectives determine it.

The superintendent will, of course, distribute the objectives. The cover letter, whether it is signed by the board president, the superintendent, or perhaps both, should cover these essential points:

- These are the *official* objectives of the school district.
- They have been adopted by the school board.
- They cannot be changed—except by the school board.
- They have been endorsed by the administration.
- They have been developed by the faculty.
- They have been endorsed by the faculty.
- They are to guide teaching.
- They will be used to evaluate learning.
- They can be learned by at least 75 percent of the students—hopefully by 100 percent, using remediation where necessary.
- They are the most important statement ever published by the school district.

- The only statement that will ever outrank them is a revised list of objectives.

Now, who are these "program designers" to whom the objectives must be sent under that cover letter? They include all of the administrators, of course, because some programs will be designed centrally for schoolwide or districtwide use. But many program design decisions will be made in individual classrooms; thus, every teacher must have a copy of the objectives, at least for the grades and subjects he or she teaches. Moreover, many program design decisions will be made in individual homes; thus, every parent must have a copy of the objectives, at least for the grades and subjects his or her child is enrolled in. In short, because most of the day-to-day decisions about how students will be taught are made by individual teachers and by individual parents, it is essential that they be given easy-to-use copies of the objectives.

Copies of Objectives for Teachers

Our experience tells us these things about the copies for teachers:

- They should be given to elementary school teachers for every subject they teach and to high school teachers for every course they teach.
- They should be readily accessible to teachers in other grades and to teachers of other subjects.

There are several reasons for this:

1. Teachers need to know how what they teach relates to what came before and what comes after.
2. They need to know how what they teach relates to what is being taught simultaneously in other subjects by other teachers.
3. They might need to review with their students what was taught in the grade before.

4. They often need to teach some students at a more or less advanced level than other students.

- They should be accompanied by a dated cover letter containing all the points cited above. The cover letter for teachers should be stapled tightly to or, better still, printed as an integral part of the objectives themselves.

   There are usually many lists of objectives floating around a school district—old lists, draft lists, tentative lists, borrowed lists, revised lists, experimental lists, incomplete lists, obsolete lists. Set the board's official list apart with a dated cover letter.

- They should be published separately from all other materials—separately from curriculum guides, course descriptions, syllabi, teachers' guides, and so on. There are several reasons for this:

   1. The objectives are the school board's, subject to change only by the board.

   2. The contents of the other publications—all 3:00 publications—should not be adopted by the board, but should be left instead to the superintendent to create and to revise at will, without the board's approval.

   3. The 12:00 objectives are more important by far than anything in the 3:00 publications—and probably more permanent.

   4. The objectives should be kept in daily view, convenient for use, study, and discussion.

- Copies of the objectives should, of course, appear in all of the 3:00 publications—and perhaps even in other publications, such as course catalogs for high school students. But it will not do to have the only copies of the board's 12:00 objectives scattered and buried in five-inch teachers' guides or in 10-volume curriculum guides. Copies must be kept on the surface as well.

- Each separate objective should be referenced to the commonly available materials used for teaching it. That will both assure teachers that materials for teaching the objectives are readily at hand and be a great convenience as they use the objectives to plan lessons. (This referencing should be done as part of the 3:00 publications since the board does not need to have or to approve the references. The superintendent must be free to change the references as needed to keep them up to date.)

Copies of Objectives for Parents

The cheapest, most effective single way to guarantee that your 12:00 objectives go into the 3:00 planning and then on into the 6:00 classrooms is to give copies of the objectives to the parents. Teachers are far more likely to teach the objectives if parents have copies—especially when parents are urged to keep those copies handy, use them to teach their own children, check off what their children are learning, and bring those copies to parent conferences with the teachers. When parents (even a small percentage of parents) use the objectives that way, they stay on top of the teachers' desks.

We say that copies of objectives for parents are one of two essential "bookends" you must use to prop up the 12:00 objectives so that they actually go into the teachers' classrooms. The other "bookend"—a far more expensive, but also more effective one—will come later on at 9:00.

Our experience tells us these things about the copies for parents:

- They should be verbatim copies of the objectives given to teachers.

- They should be printed as *checklists* so as to encourage parents to check off each objective as their child learns it.

- They should be accompanied by a dated cover letter containing all the points cited earlier. The cover letter for parents should contain these additional points:

- Parents should teach their child the objectives.

- Parents cannot expect the schools to take 100 percent of the responsibility for teaching the objectives.

- Children learn better when their parents encourage them and help them.

- Parents should check off each objective as their child learns it.

- Parents should bring their checklist to conferences with teachers to compare notes on what the child is learning.

- Parents should ask teachers to explain any objectives they do not understand.

- Parents should ask teachers to suggest how they can teach objectives to their own child at home.

• The parents' checklist of objectives should include general suggestions for parents about how they can help their children learn, such as by reading to them, taking them to the library, discussing what they are learning in school, setting up good study conditions, and checking their homework. Here are just a few examples of the suggestions sent home in the checklists of some school districts:

- Ask another adult to help you teach your child these objectives—aunt, uncle, grandparent, or neighbor.

- Show your child how you use academic skills at home in cooking, carpentry, budgeting, shopping, planning trips, and other everyday ways.

- Tell your child how you use academic skills in your job in measuring, figuring, estimating, reading, writing, speaking, hypothesizing, evaluating, and so on.

- Do mathematical puzzles and play word games with your child.

- Help your child understand charts, graphs, and maps you find in newspapers or magazines.

- Look over your child's homework papers *before* they go to school and *after* they come back home.

These are only a handful of examples from a far

longer list of suggestions. But even these few are
enough to show that the theme of the suggestions is
this: Teach your child these objectives; the schools
cannot do it all alone.

In summary, then, the only thing the school board
should do at 3:00 is to make certain that everyone who
will decide *how* to teach knows *what* to teach. The objectives adopted by you at 12:00 establish *what* to teach.
They will, in turn, guide administrators, teachers, and
parents in deciding *how* to teach. The board does not
know enough to decide how professionals should teach.
Moreover, you should not care how they teach. Once you
set the objectives for student learning at 12:00 and make
certain that clear copies are in the hands of professionals
and parents—and why not students themselves?—you
should go over to 9:00 and wait for the learning reports
to come in. Then, and only then, can you know whether
the superintendent and the others did what they should
have done at 3:00.

Curriculum Guides for Teachers

One thing the superintendent may want to do is develop curriculum guides for teachers. Most districts have
already created some form of these 3:00 documents, at
least in some grades and in some subjects, if not all. They
are most common in the elementary grades and most
common in English and mathematics, although your district may have developed them in other grades and other
subjects as well.

Curriculum guides have been around for at least a
half century, so they are no novelty. The familiar ones are
giant cookbooks of sorts, intended to help teachers by of-
fering hundreds of recipes for classroom lessons. The typical recipe stipulates an objective to be learned, suggests
at least one activity for teaching it, and points toward a

variety of materials that could or should be used in the lesson. An occasional guide goes so far as to provide a test question or some other means for determining whether the lesson worked. Such a guide becomes a giant cabinet of miniature clocks, each clock with a 12:00 objective, a 3:00 teaching activity, and a 9:00 measurement device.

Do teachers use these curriculum guides? The answer to that will have to wait until 6:00, when we describe what happens behind the classroom door, when actual teaching begins. Right now, we are at 3:00, in the world of the ideal, imagining and designing the kind of teaching we want, just as in the ideal world of 12:00 we imagined and designed the kind of learning we wanted. Stay tuned for the 6:00 news, when we report what happens when the ideal world meets the real world.

Curriculum Guides for Parents

"Parents don't know how to *teach* the objectives. Some parents can't even *understand* the objectives. We've got parents in this city who can't even *read* the objectives—even the *kindergarten* objectives. Mailing them the objectives is not enough."

A big Northern city was speaking. It was a city that had had the Federal Court looking over its shoulder for years, a court with an aggressive insistence on genuine parent involvement. Mickey Mouse techniques would not do.

We thought hard about training the parents, but there were more than 50,000 of them, even allowing only one parent for most children. And we knew from experience that—especially given the cross-city busing of children to integrate the schools—parent meetings would be hard to schedule, expensive to conduct, and poorly attended.

So we decided to create curriculum guides for parents so they could teach their children at home. Of course, we knew the guides would not help the *illiterate* parents help their children (unless relatives or churches used them, which they did), but they could help many parents help their children. Well, the guides could help if we made them good enough—say, the best parent materials ever created. That was the assignment we gave ourselves: the best in content, the best in looks. The school district agreed to supply the leadership, the staff, the money, and the courage to do something never done before; we agreed to supply the design, the technical assistance, and the quality control.

The result was the best product we have ever helped a school district create, a publication so outstanding we will put it up against anything ever published for parents by any district anywhere.

Now, if that gets your attention, here's what it looked like:

- There were nine different parent handbooks about reading, one for each grade 1-9.

- Every parent got a copy in early September, more than one copy if he or she had children in more than one grade.

- Each book had the same theme, insistently hammered out in plain talk in bold print: *Remember—the schools cannot do it all alone.*

- The superintendent opened each book with a clear message to parents:

  "Our students cannot read the way they should. This has been true for too many years. It is time to change that. But the schools cannot do it alone. Parents must help their own children as well."

- One page was headed: *What We Expect of Our Parents.* One paragraph said:

  "Reading is the most important skill your children will

ever learn. We expect you to tell your children that reading well is the key to success in school, at work, in the family, and in the society."

- One page was headed: *What We Expect of Our Students.* It named these obligations, among others:

  - Learn all of the reading skills in this book.
  - Read daily at home.
  - Try very hard on all reading tests.

- One page was headed: *What We Expect of Our Teachers.* It said that teachers must do these things, among others, for parents:

  - Teach all of the reading skills in this book to your child.
  - Use another way to teach when the first one does not work.
  - Give you helpful hints on how to help your child read.
  - Show you or your child an up-to-date record of the child's progress any time you or your child asks.

- Each book had four solid pages on how to teach, how to test, what to do with a slow child, what to do with a fast child.

- Each book listed every reading objective taught in that grade—from a minimum of 24 in grade 9 to a maximum of 54 in grade 2. (Remember that these were just the *reading* objectives—not writing, listening, speaking, or literature.)

- Each book had a separate, detailed home lesson plan for every single objective. Each lesson plan contained:

  - The objective to be learned (a verbatim copy of the one the teacher had).
  - A section titled *Explain This to Your Child*, which was actually designed to explain the objective to the parent, who could then pass the explanation along to the child.

- A section titled *Do This with Your Child*, consisting of two or three simple home teaching activities. For young children, most were games; for all children, most were hands-on tasks that required the child to be active and to do most of the work.

- A test question taken directly from the school district's 9:00 reading test for that grade.

These books were curriculum guides for parents—guides written in the belief that "parent involvement" does not mean "public relations," but rather engaging the parents directly every day in the central business of the school—teaching their children.

Since then, we expanded the idea in a Southern city. Those parent handbooks include objectives, explanations, and teaching activities for all of English (not just reading), math, science, social studies, and health in kindergarten through eighth grade. Of course, the curriculum is so extensive in those five subjects that parents get *four* handbooks per child each year—one at the beginning of *each marking period* so that they know exactly what to work on for the next nine weeks.

What do parents think of the handbooks? That school district asked 800 of them, and about 400 answered. This is what those 400 said.

Question	Answer
1. Were the handbooks valuable, useful, or informative?	97% Yes
2. Did the handbooks help you understand which objectives your child had to master?	98% Yes
3. Did you think the suggestions to parents were good?	89% Yes
4. Did you use the handbooks *frequently* to help your child?	64% Yes
5. Would you like to receive handbooks next year?	96% Yes

The results speak for themselves.

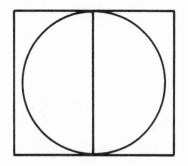

6:00   Operating
Programs

Now we are even deeper in the superintendent's territory: actual teaching. This is the very heart of professional territory.

If 3:00 is Europe, 6:00 is Russia. Here you are not merely a tourist in a foreign land, you are an unwelcome visitor in a hostile country. *Yankee Go Home.* This is the professional inner sanctum, where no board member is welcome. Teachers and administrators want school board members inside the classroom as much as surgeons want hospital board members inside the operating room. The professionals are willing to describe their operating procedures to civilians in a general way that they think civilians might understand—and hopefully admire and appreciate—but they do not want to be observed while they operate.

Try it out. Visit a classroom. As soon as you open the door, the teacher will stop teaching. The teacher will come over to greet you, chat with you, show you around, let you talk with the students—but the teacher will not actually resume teaching until you leave.

When board members "visit the schools," the professionals expect them to act like hospital board members visiting the hospital. The professionals expect board members to make "public relations rounds," not "medical rounds." They expect board members to shake hands, be interested, ask questions, find things to admire, look over the new equipment, hear about additional equipment the professionals would like to buy, hear about new staff they would like to add, go away with a favorable impression of what is happening, and resolve to do whatever they can as board members to support the activities of the professional staff—chiefly by going back to 3:00 and buying whatever the professionals have asked for during the 6:00 visit. Those welcome visits to the schools by board members are not to be confused with participation in operating the schools' programs. Operating the programs is the job of the superintendent and the other professionals.

If you cannot control teaching at 3:00 (the thesis of the last chapter), you certainly cannot control teaching at 6:00 (the thesis of this chapter). Therefore, you must control learning (the thesis of the entire book). That is the only kind of control you can get—and the only kind you need.

You must, however, understand how the superintendent should control what goes on at 6:00.

From Blueprint to Construction

If 3:00 is the plan for teaching, 6:00 is the result of the plan. If 3:00 is the blueprint, 6:00 is the building. (Teaching cannot exactly be "blueprinted"—as explained earlier at 3:00. It is an art. But it can be clearly conceived, using a set of principles.)

It goes without saying that 3:00 and 6:00 should match. Often, they do not. Most people who observe actual classroom teaching are disappointed: It does not look as good as it should. What the observer standing outside the door imagines—or hopes—will be happening is not happening when the observer gets on the other side of the classroom door.

If teachers are not teaching as they should, students will not learn as they should. When teaching falls short, learning falls short. Any shortfall at 6:00, deep in the heart of professional territory, far beyond the control of board members, will inevitably produce a shortfall at 9:00, deep in the heart of board territory—which should be well within the control of board members. When the classroom fails in September, the board room will fail in June.

If teachers cause board members to fail, it is natural for the board to try to control teaching in order to prevent that failure. But remember: You as a board member cannot control teaching, no matter how hard you try; the only thing you can control is learning. And any board that actually does control learning will lose interest in controlling teaching.

Here is an interesting question: Do teachers cause board members to fail, or do board members cause teachers to fail? The answer is that they cause each other to fail. That is what the clock means: It is a sequence of causes and effects, a series of dominoes. The first domino is the board's at 12:00. If the board pushes that domino the wrong way (or, more commonly, doesn't push it at all), no other domino can fall the right way. So ultimately, everything is the board's fault. That is what it means to govern.

Let's talk about *how* the classroom falls short at 6:00, then about *why*. The classroom often falls short in ways like these:

- Teachers spend too little time teaching. They spend too much time getting organized, doing clerical work, being interrupted, getting off the track, finding materials, or regaining control of the class.

- Students spend too little time working. They spend too much time waiting, getting organized, being interrupted, getting off the track, finding materials, or just daydreaming.

- Students are too passive, not actively engaging in the learning tasks, but listening without thinking, reading without studying, waiting for the answers rather than supplying the answers.

- Teachers teach the middle half of the class, unable to reach the top quarter or the bottom quarter.

- Things move too fast for some students, too slowly for others.

- Teachers do not know their subjects.

- Teachers cannot get their subjects across.

- Students are not sure what they are supposed to learn and remember versus what they are permitted to learn and forget, prompting the frequent question: "Will this be on the test?"

- Teachers get too few rewards, too many penalties.

- Students get too few rewards, too many penalties.

- Teachers are bored.

- Students are bored.

- Over the years, the gap widens between the good students and the poor students.

Why does this happen? One reason is at 12:00. The typical school board has not made it clear to everyone—administrators, teachers, parents, and students—what has to be learned in each grade, subject, and course. Lacking that vivid target, classes do not get off to a running start, do not move in a consistent direction, and do not sprint, but rather wander, toward a fuzzy finish line.

Another reason is at 3:00. Proper blueprints for the program are often not in place. There are three possible flaws with respect to those blueprints:

1.   *No* 3:00 blueprint—No one has decided how to teach.

2.   *Bad* 3:00 blueprints—Someone has chosen poor ways to teach.

3.   *Ignored* 3:00 blueprints—Someone has chosen good ways to teach, but no one uses them.

Let's glance at each one, because you should understand why things go wrong in the classroom, even if you cannot fix them by trying to control classroom teaching.

1. No 3:00 Blueprints

Do not be surprised if the superintendent and principals have only a fuzzy idea of what classroom teaching should look like. Just be disappointed.

Admittedly, researchers have not given administrators much help. For more than 50 years, researchers have tried to figure out which methods of teaching work. Their conclusion is: Everything works. Films work, demonstrations work, television works, discussion groups work, computers work, textbooks work, tutoring works, small groups work, large groups work. Even lectures work, much criticized though they have been in the high schools. Even workbooks work, much criticized though they have been in the elementary schools.

Given this, who can blame the administrators for saying things like:

- "Each teacher has his or her own way of doing things."
- "What works for one teacher won't work for another."
- "There is no one best method of teaching."
- "Some teachers can make *any* method work; some teachers cannot make *any* method work."
- "Teachers' methods differ as much as their personalities."
- "*Who* does the teaching matters more than *how* the teaching is done."

- "The main thing is that the teacher really likes the students."

Researchers have, in fact, come up with a few generalizations. The trouble is that they are exactly the same as the ones that Mrs. O'Leary in the house next door would have come up with—except that it would not have taken her 50 years to do it. Here are a few examples from a recent major summary of research findings:

- Children improve their reading ability by reading a lot.

- Learning to count everyday objects is an effective basis for early arithmetic lessons.

- Accomplishment in a particular activity is often more dependent upon hard work and self-discipline than on innate ability.

- Belief in the value of hard work, the importance of personal responsibility, and the importance of education itself contributes to greater success in school.

- Parental involvement helps children learn more effectively.

- When teachers explain exactly what students are expected to learn and demonstrate the steps needed to accomplish a particular academic task, students learn more.

- Memorizing can help students absorb and retain the factual information on which understanding and critical thought are based.

- The ways in which children study influence strongly how much they learn.

- Teachers can often help children develop better study habits.

- Student achievement rises significantly when teachers regularly assign homework and students conscientiously do it.

- Homework is most useful when teachers carefully prepare the assignment, thoroughly explain it, and give prompt comments and criticisms when the work is completed.

- The best way to learn a foreign language in school is to start early and to study it intensively over many years.

- The stronger the emphasis on academic courses, the more advanced the subject matter, and the more rigorous the textbooks, the more high school students learn.

- Subjects that are learned mainly in school rather than at home, such as science and math, are most influenced by the number and kind of courses taken.

- Teaching gifted students at a faster pace results in their achieving more than similarly gifted students who are taught at a normal rate.

Boring? It is almost embarrassing for leading educators to announce that researchers have once again discovered what Mrs. O'Leary already knew. Take, for example, the uncomfortable words of the U.S. Secretary of Education when he announced recently:

> "It is so well established by research and common sense as to sound foolish to repeat, but children tend to learn that which they spend time studying, and they tend to learn it in proportion to the amounts of time that they spend on it."

Or, as Mrs. O'Leary would have said, "The more you study, the more you learn."

This is the kind of announcement that causes people to question whether teaching is a profession. The members of a profession are supposed to know something that other people don't.

The researchers understand learning considerably better than they understand teaching, by the way. The easiest way to see that is to re-read the preceding list, including the Secretary's final statement. Most of these are not statements about *teaching* at all; they are statements about *learning*. You will notice that when most people try to describe good teaching techniques, they slip off into describing good learning techniques.

Why would that be? The reason is probably that the main thing the researchers have found out about learning is this:

> A student does not learn what the teacher does; a student learns what the student does.

Mrs. O'Leary could have said that, too. Of course, a psychologist would say it better. Listen to the words of Jean Piaget of Switzerland, one of the world's most respected educational psychologists:

> "The accent must be on auto-regulation, on active assimilation—the accent must be on the activity of the subject. Failing this, there is no possible didactic or pedagogy which significantly transforms the subject."

Translating freely from Piaget's French:

> "A student does not learn what the teacher does; a student learns what the student does. Any teaching method that does not get the student to study does not work."

Conversely, any method that does get the student to study, does work. Because almost any method can make students study about as well as any other method, almost any method works about as well as any other method. Or, to put it another way, some teachers can get students to study by using almost *any* method, while other teachers cannot get students to study by using almost *any* method—just as the superintendent said earlier.

In such a world, a world where everything works as well as everything else, why blueprint a method? Many superintendents and principals do not.

But no blueprint for planning teaching at 3:00 means no template for judging teaching at 6:00. So when teaching at 6:00 does not look as it should, it may be because no one has decided how it should look at 3:00.

2. Bad 3:00 Blueprints

This is easier to imagine than to demonstrate. What school district would deliberately adopt—and use—bad teaching methods? It is easier to imagine and demonstrate that there can grow up in the culture of a school an unofficial, but influential, set of ideas that makes bad teaching acceptable and a matching set of habits that makes it pervasive.

- Picture an elementary school of low-achieving minority children from broken homes, a faculty that has given up hope that the children can ever achieve like those across town, and a principal who rarely leaves the office. A school like that can breed the acceptability of pedestrian teaching. Worse yet, such a school can extinguish enthusiasm and even hope in the occasional bright-eyed new teacher, slowly imposing the faculty's habit of lazy, uninspired teaching on that person's behavior, until the newcomer conforms or gets out.

- Picture a middle school in a neighborhood with a highly mobile population, student turnover so rapid that teachers can scarcely meet parents before they move away, a sequential curriculum designed for a stable student body, a principal preoccupied with discipline, and a faculty whose objective is to get through the day without jarring incidents and whose method is tight control of classroom behavior. A school like that can substitute procedures designed to control student behavior for procedures designed to produce student learning.

- Picture a high school in which the faculty believes that the students are almost old enough to go to college and should be taught as if they were already there. The faculty members, who would like to be college professors themselves, believe that the high school should be run like a cafeteria line: Teachers serve up their subjects; students go through the line one time, and they get the stuff or they don't. No spoon feeding—just like college. The principal agrees. A school like that can cause teachers to march through the objectives—or the pages of the textbook—regardless of whether students follow.

What these bad blueprints, these habits of mind, have in common is hopelessness—the assumption that many of the students cannot, or will not, learn. That is, please note yet again, an assumption about learning, not an actual teaching technique.

We might say that what makes a teaching technique bad is the assumption that it is not going to work—not because the technique itself is bad, but because the students are bad. The logical converse would be that what makes a teaching technique good is the assumption that it is going to work—not because the technique itself is remarkable, but simply because the students are good. That would mean that what radiates through every good teaching technique is the teacher's faith (and that is exactly the right word) that the students can and will learn.

That faith is what makes the technique work. Why? Because the students see the faith shining through the technique, adopt the faith (that is, literally adopt the belief in themselves), and try—whereupon they succeed. As Piaget said, any method that does not get students to try does not work. Any method used by a teacher who believes in the students will work, because the students are moved by the belief more than by the method. And vice versa.

Thus, a bad blueprint for a teaching method is anything describing a method teachers think will not work with their students. Mrs. O'Leary could have said that. This is why superintendents fret so much about establishing "ownership" of a new program among teachers. Superintendents know that if teachers think something won't work, why, surely enough, it won't. No surprise there.

3. Ignored 3:00 Blueprints

Those overstuffed 3:00 "curriculum guides" that have to be brought into the board room by wheelbarrow are famous for something other than their weight. Those elaborate cookbooks with hundreds of recipes for tasty classroom lessons are most famous for being ignored.

Nobody thinks they control teaching; many people think they scarcely influence teaching—especially beyond grade 5 or 6. Few things get as much blood, sweat, and tears put into them and give back so little benefit in return. Why is this? Curriculum guides seem like such a good idea—indeed, such an essential idea. Get a representative group of teachers together, have them decide both what and how to teach, cite the materials to use, maybe even the means of measurement—and publish the results for all teachers. Why don't teachers use those guides? Here are some of the reasons:

1. Curriculum guides are an administrator's idea, not a teacher's. Even though every word in them may be written by classroom teachers, they are a bureaucratic tool, not a professional tool. They are supplied by administrators, but they are not demanded by teachers. Their chief function is to impress outsiders, such as board members, that the classrooms are under administrative control.

2. Once developed, they are not enforced. Deliberately labelled "guides" and filled with "suggested" teaching activities, they are draped with apologies for their presumptuous administrative invasion of professional territory. Administrators treat them as optional teaching devices; teachers treat them as optional administrative advice. Administrators never use them to observe, and certainly not to evaluate, classroom teaching.

3. Teachers do not really agree about how to teach. They believe, along with everybody else, that any method works or that many methods work. Thus, what teachers owe each other is not printed advice about how to teach, but senatorial courtesy. That is: "You teach your way, and I'll teach mine." To refer a colleague to the curriculum guide would be, well, rude.

4. Teachers are intuitive cooks, not recipe readers. Veterans use a dash of this, a pinch of that, stirring as the class bubbles along, tasting, watching, adding the seasonings of their own seasoning. Beginners were never taught to read recipes in their teachers' colleges, so they teach as they were taught or learn to cook through classroom trial and error.

5. Teachers think that being a professional means making up your own techniques, not following well-established, widely-accepted professional behaviors. In this, teachers differ from accountants, anthropologists, architects, attorneys, dentists, engineers, ministers, and statisticians. That is, teachers see themselves more as artists than as applied scientists. Engineers use handbooks; teachers do not use curriculum guides.

6. Textbooks overpower all other blueprints for teaching school. These remarkably complete containers of 12:00 objectives, 3:00 techniques and materials, and 9:00 test questions placed in the hands of a 6:00 teacher are irresistibly sufficient to operate the day, the week, the semester, the year. They become the curriculum guides.

Whatever the reasons, the curriculum in print is rarely the curriculum in fact. The best blueprints will not control what the contractor does on the job, and the best curriculum guide will not control what the teacher does in the classroom. But that should not trouble you as a board member. You know that you cannot control teaching; you can control only learning.

Supervision as a Method for Controlling 6:00

What about supervision? Isn't supervision what makes contractors follow blueprints? Can't it be used to make actual teaching look like ideal teaching? Can't it be used to make 6:00 match 3:00?

The first answers that occur to us are variations of: Are you serious? Be serious. Did you ever go to school? But the innocent question deserves a real answer. And a good answer begins with a definition:

> Supervision is the over-the-shoulder prevention of mistakes.

Supervision must not be mistaken for evaluation. Evaluation is something else entirely:

> Evaluation is finding mistakes after they have been made.

You can see the difference: Supervision prevents mistakes; evaluation finds mistakes. A traffic cop supervises traffic to prevent mistakes, not to discover them. An auditor, on the other hand, checks financial records to discover mistakes, not to prevent them. Both are useful, but different.

We need one more concept about supervision before we can talk about the supervision of teaching. It's a highly objectionable concept, a deeply disappointing concept. Most board members and professionals do not like this concept, but they do agree with it:

You cannot supervise what you cannot do.

There are two powerful reasons why that is true:

1. A supervisor who does not know all the ways things can go wrong cannot prevent every single one of them from going wrong. That is exactly what any good supervisor must do: anticipate every mistake and order the moves necessary to prevent it. For example, don't allow more cars into an intersection than can get out of it. And remember that engines die, brakes fail, drivers drink, and some people don't pay attention. These things are best learned by driving.

2. No worker will take instruction from a person who cannot do the job. The only exception would be a worker who deliberately wants to make trouble by taking advice he knows will do damage: "Okay. Okay! I'll do it your way. Remember: You asked for it." Crash!

Now, knowing that supervision is done to prevent mistakes and you cannot supervise what you cannot do, let's talk about administrative supervision as a method for controlling 6:00 teaching.

We run workshops for board members in which we ask if any board member has ever had a paid job other than teaching. The board members name their paid jobs: office manager, lawyer, insurance salesperson, programmer, engineer, carpenter, exporter, farmer, librarian, undertaker, vice president, druggist—whatever.

Next, we ask whether any board member has ever given or received supervision (mistake prevention by someone who could do the job). Most say:

"Yes."

Then we ask how often. Board members usually say:

"Weekly."

"Daily."

"Hourly."

"Continuously."

Finally, we change the scene to the classrooms in their school districts. We ask them to pick any school, any grade, any subject, any teacher. Then we say:

"Now, open the door to the classroom, go inside, close the door quietly behind you, and stand facing it. Look at your watch. How long will you have to wait inside that classroom before a supervisor comes through the door—a supervisor who comes in to prevent mistakes, a supervisor who could teach that class? Look at your watch. Oh. You need a calendar?"

Board members usually say:

"A couple of months."

"Six months."

"A year."

"Ten years."

"Forever."

With such answers, board members (and their superintendents, who frequently attend the workshops) have taught us that there is no supervision in the public schools of this country, no mistake prevention.

Once we were leading a statewide workshop for board members in Missouri. They were not happy. We had just defined supervision, and they did not like the definition.

They: Principals in my district do the supervising.

We: Can they teach the classes they visit?

They: Well, no. They haven't had experience in every grade and every subject. So, of course, they can't teach all the classes. They just supervise.

We: You cannot supervise what you cannot do.

They: Under that definition, there is no supervision whatever in the Missouri public schools.

We: You said it first.

They: But what about visiting classrooms to make sure teachers are teaching, there is good order, and kids are working? *Any* good principal can do that.

We: That is *evaluating discipline*, not supervising the teaching of algebra or kindergarten music or fifth grade physical education.

They: We like to think of our principals as the instructional leaders in the buildings.

We: Leaders they may be; supervisors they are not. You cannot supervise what you cannot do.

They: Well, that standard is too high for Missouri. Be realistic. Give us some practical standard we can use for principals.

Now there was a challenge. Principals didn't know enough to teach the classes in their schools. Their board members had just established that. We needed a lower standard for principals—a kind of minimum competency level before they could be allowed to go into the classrooms. But not too low. These were, after all, Missouri's "principal" teachers. Yet not too high, or we would rob Missouri schools of their leaders. What to suggest? Then came an idea:

"All right. Here it is. You may think this is too low. Try to think of it instead as a modern Missouri Compromise. The principal has to pass every test administered in the school."

Most board members frowned; some laughed; one cried. We had to leave town.

But to this day, we think that is reasonable. A school principal should know as much as the students in the school. Otherwise, how can he or she lead the teachers?

Some board members have told us that their assistant principals supervise, or the central office coordinators, or their mentor teachers, or their department chairpersons, or other teachers. But that turns out to be not true when probed. The fact is that there is no supervision in the American public schools. Every school child knows that—and every board member who has been a school child knows that. No other adult is in the classroom to prevent the teacher from making mistakes—not once a week, not once a month, not once a year. Think back to when you were a student yourself—in any grade, in any subject, in any classroom. How often did you see another adult in the classroom watching over the teacher?

Many board members have told us that their schools have *evaluation* observations (not to be confused with *supervisory* observations)—once a year in some districts, twice a year in others, even four times a year in some— usually for beginning teachers on probation, sometimes for veteran teachers on tenure. But we brush that aside, because we are talking about supervision, not evaluation.

And so the answer to the question asked earlier is "no." Supervision cannot be used to make actual 6:00 teaching look like ideal 3:00 teaching. There is no supervision.

How about evaluation? No. All evaluation can do is what it has always done: tell us that what the evaluator sees at 6:00 is a very pale copy of what she imagined—or hoped—would be happening, based on what she envisioned back at 3:00.

So, to repeat once more, you as a board member cannot control teaching through curriculum guides, training, supervision, evaluation, or any other device. Not to worry, though. All you have to do is control learning. And so we bid farewell to Russia at 6:00, just as we did to Europe at 3:00, and head for home at 9:00. It will be good to get back to where board members belong. The superintendent's territory is a nice place to visit, but you wouldn't want to live there. It is more satisfying to live where you can control things, the most important things, like learning.

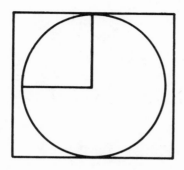

9:00 Measuring Goals and Objectives

Now it's 9:00—time to determine whether students have learned the goals and objectives you set for them at 12:00. We are moving squarely back into school board territory on the "learning" side of the fence—the side that you should control.

Just as you did not personally write the 12:00 goals and objectives for students, you will not write the 9:00 tests of those goals and objectives, either. Instead you will tell the superintendent what you will accept as proof that students have learned what you called for at 12:00. If you think about 12:00 as the order you placed with the chef, you can think about 9:00 as looking over the dishes the chef sent to your table to see whether you got what you ordered. In most cases, the proof of the 6:00 pudding will be students' scores on 9:00 tests—tests that measure the 12:00 goals and objectives.

As we pointed out in the 12:00 chapter, you will not really be measuring the *goals* at 9:00. Goals are too broad to be measured. They contain too many possible objectives. Rather, you will be measuring the nitty-gritty *objectives* you selected to define your broad goals.

As you know from 12:00, those objectives will be written for every grade and every subject in your district. There will be thousands of them. How can you test them?

Dare We Say "Test"?

To keep the language simple, we want to use the word "test" to describe what you should do at 9:00. Otherwise, we will have to use multisyllabic words like *assessment*, *appraisal*, *evaluation*, *examination*, *measurement*, *judgment*, and others favored by professional educators.

But saying "test" gives us two problems:

> *Problem 1.* You might think only of something simple like a paper-and-pencil "true-false" test.
>
> *Problem 2.* Many professional educators do not like to "test" student learning; they prefer to "assess" it or "evaluate" it or to use "criterion-referenced measurement" or something like that.

Let's solve those two problems so we can say "test" throughout this chapter.

Problem 1. This is not really a problem. You know that "test" does not always mean something simple like "true-false." We want to use "test" the way you use it outside of school board meetings, as in:

> Send this specimen over to the lab for a test.
>
> Harry, you're always testing the limits around here.
>
> This is going to be a test case.
>
> Could you test my anti-freeze level?
>
> The way he approaches that customer is going to be a test of his judgment.
>
> The county primary will be her first test.
>
> Why are you testing me this way?
>
> Gladys will give you a typing test and then you'll be finished.
>
> If she meets the September quota, I'll say she passed the test.
>
> Let me do a compression test first.
>
> You're testing my patience.

We mean what you mean. To "test" is to find out whether. And there are many ways to test—including paper-and-pencil "true-false." So when we say "test" in this chapter, you'll know that we mean finding out—somehow—whether students have learned.

Problem 2. Now this really is a problem: Many professional educators do not like to "test" student learning. They will say things to you like:

"We do too much testing."

"We are teaching many things you cannot test."

"We are so busy testing we have no time left to teach."

"Tests make students anxious."

"The most important things they learn cannot be tested."

"If we make too much of tests, we'll just encourage cheating."

"Some students cannot show what they have learned on a test. But they could show it some other way."

"Any good teacher can tell whether a student has learned something. We don't need a test."

Opposition to testing is not just a matter of individual professional opinion. Some local teachers' unions are opposed to testing; some state teachers' associations are opposed to testing; some national teachers' groups are opposed to testing. So the people who work for you have good support from their professional colleagues in opposing testing.

Now watch for a complete reversal: Actually, professional educators are not opposed to testing. You know that because you went to school. Classroom teachers test all the time—every day, every week, every marking period, every semester, every year. They test by asking questions in class, using quizzes, watching students perform, grading homework, giving exams, reading term papers, inspecting student products, and so on. And they have good reasons:

- Teachers could not teach if they could not test. Without knowing whether students had learned the last thing, teachers could not go on to the next thing.

- Teachers could not grade students and fill out report cards if they did not test.

- Teachers could not justify the grades on those report cards if they did not have test scores to back them up.

- Students might not learn if teachers did not test. Teachers commonly use a coming test to stimulate (threaten?) students to study harder:

"Final's on Friday; better get this down right."

No, professional educators are not opposed to giving tests, despite all their talk about too much testing. Then what is the problem? The problem is that many of them are opposed to *having outsiders*—like you—*get the results*. That is different from being opposed to testing, but there is a connection: If they do not *have* the results, they cannot give them to the board. So if they can persuade you not to test, you cannot get the results.

Now watch for the next reversal: Actually, professional educators are not opposed to having outsiders—like you—get the test results. They bring the board the results of national tests and state tests every year. They bring in scores expressed as stanines, standard scores, scale scores, percentiles, grade equivalents, probability bands, and gain scores. Then what is the problem? The problem is that many of them are opposed to *having outsiders*—like you—*use the results*. If you can understand them, you can use them. So they have to convince you that the results have no meaning. The sophisticated way to do this is not to claim that the results of national and state tests mean *nothing*, but to claim that they could mean *anything*. Uncertainty is enough to render you impotent.

Numerous lines of argument are used to rob national and state test results of certainty:

1. *The test questions are no good.*

   "A lot of the questions test really low-level thinking."

   "Some of the questions are tricky."

   "It's not really a science test; it's really a reading test. Students may know the science answers, but they cannot read the test questions."

2. *Some other test is better.*

   "We would really prefer to use CTBS."

   "My own feeling is that the Iowa is a better designed test."

   "When I was in New Mexico, we used STEP, which I felt gave better results."

3. *The statistics are no good.*

   "These grade equivalents really don't mean what you might think."

   "Percentiles are really misleading at these levels. Raw scores give a better picture."

   "Other districts are getting odd results, too. We called the state education department, but nobody knows why."

4. *The test is too short.*

   "There are not enough questions on each objective to tell whether a student knows the objective."

5. *The test is too long.*

   "We have to quit teaching for two or three days just to give these tests."

6. *The test is too old.*

   "This edition was normed back in 1977. A lot of things have changed since then."

7. *The test is too new.*

   "It's the first time we've given these, you know. It'll take a couple more years for teachers to get used to them. Then we'll know where we really stand."

8. *The new test does not match the old test.*

"We have not been able to find out how our scores on the new test relate to our scores on the old test. The company can't say. So we really don't know if we did better or worse this year than last year."

9. *The test does not match our curriculum.*

"They test things in grade three that we don't teach 'til grade four."

10. *The test questions don't match our test questions.*

"One difference is that they have the kids pick out misspelled words from a printed list. When we test, we have the kids actually spell out the words correctly. That's really a different kind of question."

11. *The test does not match our district.*

"Well, you have to remember that this is a state test, designed for the average district in the state. We are really nothing like the average district."

12. *The answer sheets are a problem.*

"Our teachers feel that those machine-scorable answer sheets are very confusing, especially for the younger children."

13. *The English language is a problem.*

"We have more and more students who cannot read English well enough to score well. If the tests were in their native language, who knows how well they would do?"

14. *Students' attitudes are a problem.*

"What our teachers find today is that students no longer take tests seriously—maybe because there are so many tests. They draw pictures on the test papers, write silly answers, don't even bother to finish."

15. *Other school districts cheat.*

"I can tell you this: When we saw the scores from some of the other districts, we wondered how they even got them, knowing what those districts are like."

16. *The test won't help teachers.*

"The results won't help our teachers because...."

The only thing stronger than the arguments professional educators make against national and state tests are the arguments you can make in favor of them:

"We must use *something* to compare ourselves to outsiders."

"Teach our students whatever they need in order to do well on national and state tests. We've already included all those things in our 12:00 objectives."

"We consider national and state tests to be low hurdles. Our students should jump them easily."

"As soon as professional educators develop better tests, we'll use them. Meantime, we'll use these."

Points To Keep in Mind

Testing is perhaps the most complex, most controversial topic in education. Here are a few major pointers to guide you as a civilian.

Tests as a Heavy Bookend. Calling for tests to be given to measure each 12:00 objective is the best way to make certain that the 12:00 objectives will really be used by classroom teachers to guide their daily instruction. Such 9:00 tests are the second "bookend" that you must use to prop up the objectives. (You will recall that the first "bookend," discussed at 3:00, was the issuing of parent checklists of the objectives and, if possible, parent handbooks designed to help parents teach their children the objectives.) While tests are far more expensive and more logistically difficult both to create and to use than parent materials, they are also far more powerful as a means of getting your 12:00 objectives into the classroom.

Measuring versus Judging. Although we have called this chapter "Measuring Goals and Objectives," you need to understand that there are some objectives you will place at 12:00 that cannot be *measured*, but must be *judged* instead. For example, how high a student can high jump can be measured, but how well she performs a routine on the balance beam must be judged. Whether a student knows the five-kingdom classification system can be measured, but whether she can build an interesting and accurate science fair project must be judged. Qualified outsiders can act as judges (ideal, but not realistic), or your own teachers can act as judges (not as good, but realistic). Either way, the judgments must be recorded.

The important point is that all of your 12:00 objectives should be measured or judged and that you should get the results of those measurements and judgments.

Choosing Multiple-Choice Tests. Most of your 12:00 objectives can, in fact, be measured by paper-and-pencil multiple-choice tests—the quickest and cheapest 9:00 method available. Thus, to save on the expense of gathering 9:00 evidence, use paper-and-pencil multiple-choice tests as often as you can.

Many teachers and administrators will tell you that you cannot use paper-and-pencil multiple-choice tests to measure the attitudes or high-level thinking objectives that you put at 12:00. That is not true. Attitudes can be tested using a variety of attitude questionnaires, which are easy to create and easy to administer and which will give an accurate measure of students' attitudes toward whatever you called for at 12:00. As for measuring high-level thinking, tell your staff to get a copy of a state bar exam, or the College Board's Advanced Placement tests in a variety of subjects, or even some of the commercially-produced national tests used in thousands of disticts nationwide from elementary school through high school. All of these tests contain excellent examples of high-level thinking tested with paper-and-pencil multiple-choice test questions. Ask to see the copies of the tests, and you'll see what we mean.

Three Kinds of Tests: Local, State, and National. We believe that school boards should ask their superintendents for two kinds of proof that students have learned what they were supposed to: (1) test scores on locally-developed tests built to match the school district's own 12:00 objectives (we will call them here "local tests"); and (2) test scores from any one of the widely-used commercially-produced standardized tests used in districts nationwide (we will call them here "national tests"). These two different types of tests will give you two different types of information about what students are learning. Together, they will give you the best possible handle on how your curriculum is working.

Before we talk in detail about local and national tests, let's say a word about state tests, which are produced under the auspices of the state education department and used in districts across the state on either a voluntary or a mandatory basis. If state tests are mandatory in your state, look at the results carefully to see how your students stack up with the students in other districts, both those districts comparable to your own and those that you feel may be better or worse than your own. If state tests are optional and if you have limited time and money to spend at 9:00, spend it on local tests and national tests instead. The national tests will give you the same kind of comparisons that state tests do, but on a larger scale. As mobile as our society is today, your job must be to prepare students for life in these United States, not just for life in your state. That's why a national test is a better yardstick.

Local Tests

"Local tests" aren't the things each teacher invents (or selects) to test his or her own students. Let's call those "teacher-made tests." As you know from going to school, the way those tests are created and used differs from school to school, teacher to teacher, course to course, class to class, and even student to student. The results can never be compared and can never be accumulated to tell the school board what students are learning.

We mean tests to help the board govern. Probably we should call them something like "school district tests" or "school board tests." They have to be built to high standards; they have to be used uniformly and honestly throughout the school district; and the results have to be simple, clear, and perfectly understandable to civilians.

As we have said, your local tests at 9:00 must match your local objectives at 12:00—and match them perfectly. Where would you get such tests?

There are four possibilities: one silly, two sensible, and one best. They are:

1. Pick the tests first and write the objectives second, moving backward around the clock from 9:00 to 12:00.

2. Send your objectives outside to some place that will write questions to match.

3. Buy national "banks" of test questions and search through them for questions to match your objectives.

4. Have your teachers write the questions.

1. Pick the Tests First. Silly. No professional educators alive—including yours—would agree with that. It violates every professional standard for curriculum development, runs the clock backward, would give you a narrow curriculum, guarantees that your teachers will think you want them to "teach to the test" (the ultimate professional "no-no"), and guarantees that your administrators will suspect you care more about good scores than about learning.

Actually, this silly approach is not as silly as what school boards do now: They have no local tests at all.

2. Send Your Objectives Out. Sensible. Expensive, but sensible. The advantages are speed, fewer headaches for your administrators, and less strain for your teachers. The chief disadvantage, apart from cost, is that you cannot be sure you will get high quality questions matching your objectives—especially if you hold down the price. Good questions are expensive.

3. Buy National "Banks." Sensible. This is less expensive than sending your objectives out, but slower, riskier, and more work for your own personnel. They will have to sift through thousands of questions—perhaps 100,000—trying to match your objectives. Their greatest temptation will be settling for near misses—questions that don't really match, but are the closest they can find. The results of that will be low test scores because students were taught some Civil War battles, but tested on others. You'll think the curriculum is not working, when it is the test that is not working.

4. Have Your Teachers Write the Questions. Best. Your best teachers wrote the objectives; now have them write test questions to match. Not only is this the best method, but it also costs less than sending your objectives out. Its chief merit is the "ownership" teachers feel:

The questions in the local school district tests are ones they wrote themselves. No other method does this, even when teachers are asked to review and approve questions brought in from the outside—whether the outsiders tailor-made them for the district or the district took them out of a "bank."

Having teachers write the local test questions will turn out to be extremely important later if test scores turn out to be low. If that happens, you don't want teachers finding fault with the tests. Instead, you will want to be in a position to find fault with whatever happened at 3:00 and at 6:00. Shifting the fault to the professional side of the clock is the *only* way to improve learning next year. The board president can say to the professional staff:

> "You wrote the objectives, so they are all right. You wrote the test questions, so they are all right.
>
> "There's no problem at 12:00 and 9:00, on our side of the fence. Must be at 3:00 and/or 6:00 on your side. Please fix it."

Unfortunately, having teachers write the questions for the local test has one serious drawback. Many teachers are not qualified to write good test questions.

First, most teachers have not had any technical training in writing test questions. That problem may be surmountable, but only with time, money, and effort. You will have to give them technical training, perhaps a substantial amount. If you do not have a testing and research staff in your district, you will have to employ outside consultants.

Second, and much more important, many teachers have only a loose grasp of the actual content of the 12:00 objectives. We repeatedly find that many teachers simply do not know their subjects well enough to write clear and correct test questions. This problem is much harder to surmount. You can, over the long haul, make sure that any district teacher training program you provide deals more with the content of their subjects than with methods for teaching their subjects. Many teachers already know much more about *how* to teach than they do about *what* to teach. But what can you do in the short haul so that they can write satisfactory test questions?

Here is a thumbnail sketch of the best plan we know for having your teachers produce your 9:00 questions:

1. *Choose your smartest, most literate teachers* from each grade and subject to do the test question writing. Intelligence means more than experience here. No amount of teaching experience can substitute for raw intelligence when it comes to doing this task.

2. *Hold a test question writing workshop* in which teachers get both initial training and over-the-shoulder supervision as they begin to write the test questions. This workshop should last at least one day.

3. *Set up a careful test question review process* something like this: (1) one teacher writes a test question; (2) another teacher of that grade and subject reviews and edits the test question; and (3) a central office supervisor in that subject (if you have one) reviews and edits the test question. That is probably the best *internal* district mechanism you can come up with.

4. *Have the test questions edited by someone outside the district* who can be totally objective in dealing with the teachers and their supervisors and with the flaws in their questions. This outsider might be from a nearby university, from another school district, or from an organization like ours. The outsider must be able to edit the test questions both for content mistakes and for technical mistakes. In other words, the outsider must know more about the subject than your teachers do and more about test construction than your teachers do. No amount of internal review of test questions can substitute for this kind of *external* review.

5. *Try out the questions* with students if time and money permit—but they usually do not. Pilot testing at its

simplest means that you should try the questions out with your own students to see if the questions work well. Your own testing and research staff, if you have one, should know how to do this. If not, an outside consultant can advise you on a simple pilot testing procedure.

Everyone into the Pool. Now you have some test questions matched to each of your objectives. What do you do with them? You do not type them up into a *test*. Instead, you create a district *pool* of test questions. From that pool, you will draw *many* local district tests.

The greatest advantage to having a pool of test questions for each objective is that when you give local district tests—be they at the beginning of the year, during the year at the end of each marking period, or at the end of the year—you never need to give the same test twice. Suppose you were giving end-of-year final exams, for example. Each spring the board president (or a student or the superintendent or a computer) would reach into the pool of questions blindfolded and draw out several for each objective. Those would become the final exam for that spring.

No one would know in advance what questions would be on the final exam—not the board, not the administrators, not the teachers, not the parents, not the students. (Conversely, everyone would know in advance which *objectives* would be tested: all of the objectives, every spring, no matter which final exam questions were drawn.)

Every spring, you would draw out a different handful for each objective. This means you would never have to worry about students or teachers keeping a copy of the final exam in order to be better prepared for next year. Next spring's final exam wouldn't be the same.

How many questions would you need in the test for

each of the objectives? This is as much a matter of common sense as of statistics. If you ask a student one question on an objective and the student gets the question right, can you be sure that the student knows the objective? Probably not, because the student might have been lucky and guessed the right answer. If you ask a student two questions on an objective and he gets one right and one wrong, does he know the objective? Probably not, you would say. If you ask a student three questions on an objective and he gets two right and one wrong, does he know the objective? He's getting closer. If you ask a student four questions on an objective and he gets three right and one wrong, does he know the objective? Most board members, by common sense, would say "yes" and settle for that as a standard. In other words, if you want to make sure that a student knows an objective and you ask him four questions about it and he gets three right, you would settle. You would not insist on four out of five or five out of six. So four questions per objective are enough.

If you did not care whether *each* student had learned each separate objective, but rather whether most students were learning most social studies objectives in fifth grade, you could get by with *fewer* than four questions per objective. And you would have a much shorter test. But to help teachers pick out and reteach individual students on individual objectives, four questions per objective are the ideal. You will have a much longer test, of course. That's the trade-off.

A pool has many other uses—if it is deep enough. Let's say that your district had 10 test questions matched to each 12:00 objective. That would be a deep pool. Think of the possibilities:

1. Give one question per objective to *teachers* to help clarify exactly what each objective means.

2.   Give one question per objective to *parents* to help clarify the objectives so that they can teach their children and/or test their children.

3.   Give one question per objective to *students* so that they will have a better idea of what target they are trying to hit—and whether they are hitting it.

4.   Use several questions per objective in a districtwide test in each subject and grade at the *beginning* of the school year to show teachers exactly what their students do and do not already know so that their teaching can be focused accordingly.

5.   Use several questions per objective in a districtwide test in each subject and grade at the end of each marking period *during* the year so that teachers, administrators, and you as a board member can monitor students' progress throughout the year.

6.   Use several questions per objective in a districtwide final exam in each subject and grade at the *end* of the year so that teachers, administrators, and you as a board member can judge how much students remember when the year is over.

7.   Print one question per objective in the local *newspaper* to show your taxpayers how much learning they are getting for their money.

     One advantage of printing the questions is that you can invite (challenge?) taxpayers to answer them. Some won't get past fifth grade, demonstrating how much you are teaching your students. (Be sure to print the correct answers, too.)

     You can achieve some of the same effect by printing the *objectives* in the newspaper. Or you can print both.

A final advantage of a deep pool is that you can forget about keeping tests "secure"—that is, preventing people from getting copies. That is almost impossible, anyway. Besides, teachers can resent "test security" as not trusting their professional integrity. A deep pool makes it unnecessary.

What would happen if a teacher got the entire pool and then taught the students the answers to all of the test questions—all 10 for each objective? What would happen? By the time the teacher taught the students all the answers to all the questions in the entire pool, the students would know all the objectives. For example, imagine a teacher teaching students the answers to 10 test questions on capitalizing the names of cities and states. By the time the students were taught to capitalize the names of cities and states correctly in all 10 questions in the pool, they would probably be able to capitalize the names of cities and states anywhere, any time.

So go ahead and give teachers—and anybody else— the entire pool, if it is deep enough. Invite teachers to swim around in it all year, using some of the questions for their daily quizzes and weekly tests rather than writing their own. Using the pool will save teachers time, and the pool questions will be better than what most teachers would write on their own. Most important, the students will always be shooting at the same target: the objectives described by the district's pool of questions.

You can't lose with a deep pool of test questions. And neither can the teachers. And neither can the students.

Advantages of Local Tests

Because a local testing program is expensive to create and expensive to operate, there should be substantial advantages to justify the cost. Here are some of the most important ones.

1. The 9:00 Test Matches the 12:00 Objectives. An

explanation teachers and administrators often give for not doing well on national tests is that the national 9:00 tests include questions on objectives that are not part of your 12:00 curriculum. In other words, the national tests examine students on things that they were never taught. You can get rid of that explanation by using your own local tests. Your local 9:00 test is a perfect match for your own 12:00 objectives. Every single one of the objectives tested by your local test is an objective that teachers knew perfectly well they were supposed to teach—because you printed and distributed the full 12:00 set. Therefore, if students do not score well on your local tests, it is not because the test does not match the objectives. The fault lies at 3:00 and/or 6:00.

2. You Can Test All Subjects in All Grades. If you create local tests, you can—and should—have a local test for every grade and every subject. You should have a local districtwide test for tenth grade art, fourth grade music, seventh grade physical education, twelfth grade physics, kindergarten social studies, fifth grade mathematics—and every other grade and subject. As we said earlier, if something is worth spending taxpayers' money and students' time to teach, it is worth spending a little more of them to see whether students actually learned it.

If you are using national tests now, and you almost certainly are, find out what they test. You may test certain subjects only (most likely English and math) and certain grades only (something like grades 3, 6, and 9).

Have you ever talked to teachers about that? They sometimes say things to us like, "Why aren't the social studies and science teachers ever on the hook? Why just English and math? And what about seventh grade teachers? The district never tests seventh grade. Why just us?" In other words, if you use only national tests, many—if not most—of the teachers in your district probably escape having their work inspected against any outside standard.

If you believe that using the results of tests can actually help teachers teach better (we do), you will want your art teachers, music teachers, physical education teachers, vocational education teachers, and all other teachers in every grade to have such results. No set of national tests can supply results for all of your teachers. You must do that with your own local tests.

3. You Can Test During the Year and Make Improvements Before June. If you use your local tests at the end of each marking period or each semester, you won't have to be surprised in June by the bad news that students did not learn everything you had imagined at 12:00. You can do something about it before June. For example, let's say that there are 20 social studies objectives assigned to each of four marking periods in fifth grade. Your superintendent would produce a local test for the first 20 social studies objectives for the first marking period, test your fifth graders in November, and give the results to you in December. That way, both you and the superintendent would know whether teachers and students were getting the job done—early enough for the superintendent to take immediate corrective action if needed.

We once worked on the West Coast in a rural district so small that the superintendent himself used local test scores during the year to pay attention to student learning. He called in the eighth grade math teacher one time to have him explain why the November scores on the local tests were so low.

"The math textbook I use in eighth grade doesn't have all the objectives in it," the teacher explained.

"I studied the math objectives before I called you in," the superintendent responded. "Leon, I could teach them myself with a piece of chalk. Until we can afford new math textbooks, that's what I want you to do. These are the board's objectives, and we have to teach them. Come back in February and let's have a look at the second marking period scores."

Do you think that is too much intervention—or exactly what you wish would happen in your district? The point is that local testing during the year at 9:00 in your territory enables the administration to make midcourse corrections in its territory. Since you don't have any supervision (as we explained at 6:00), you may want this kind of frequent evaluation.

As for Leon, he can look at the November test scores objective by objective, pinpoint the trouble, and reteach the unlearned objectives early in the second marking period.

4. There Is No Good Way To "Teach to the Test." We already made this point when we described the power of having a pool of test questions for each objective. Because there is not one test for second grade math that is given every year, but rather a pool of test questions from which many different tests might be assembled, there is no way that teachers can "teach to the test"—a popular worry among educators.

They might "teach to the pool" of test questions, but there are so many in the pool—say 10 questions for each objective, making a pool of hundreds in each grade and subject—that teaching to the pool would be very difficult.

What teachers must teach to instead are your 12:00 objectives—the ones on which the 9:00 tests are based—because that works better than teaching the answers to 10 different questions on each objective. The best defense against teaching to the test is a good offense: a pool of test questions.

5. The 12:00 Objectives Get Better. There is no better way to clean up and clarify the 12:00 objectives—preferably while they are being written or before they are made final—than to have your own teachers write 9:00 test questions to match them. Through writing the 9:00 test questions, teachers themselves will come to understand the 12:00 objectives far better. They will then be able to refine the objectives so that they are perfectly clear before they come to you for adoption. If they are clear to you as a civilian, they will then be clear to teachers and parents.

6. Teacher Training Needs Are Revealed. As we explained earlier, when teachers write the test questions, it will become clear to your outside editors (and to your inside administrators) just what teachers do not know. For example, we once had a group of English teachers write test questions on "foreshadowing" in literature. The committee turned in about 20 questions. Not one had any foreshadowing in it. That foreshadowed a much-needed teacher training program.

Nothing in our experience had foreshadowed that having local teachers write local test questions would reveal what teachers did know and didn't know about their subjects. We never saw that coming. Gradually, we came to realize that just as a student who doesn't know the subject can't answer the questions, a teacher who doesn't know the subject can't write them. Today we think that the very best way to design a teacher training program in subject content (not in teaching methods) is to have teachers write test questions and to see what content mistakes they are making.

What other way do you have? Your administrators don't supervise—and if they did, it would probably be only for classroom control and teaching methods. They don't test teachers on subject content *before* they hire them. They certainly don't do it *after* they hire them. Students can't tell. Parents don't know. We cannot think of a time when a teacher displays his or her knowledge of the subject before a professional audience in as much detail as when he or she is writing test questions. Writing objectives, we have found, does not reveal nearly so well what the teacher knows about the subject. Their objectives don't foreshadow their test questions. We have finally figured out why: A teacher has to know 16 times as much about the subject to write four good four-part multiple-choice tests questions as to write one objective.

7. No One Else Can Be Blamed for Poor Test Results. Politically speaking, this is the most powerful advantage to local tests created by your own teachers at 9:00. If students do not do well on local tests, teachers cannot say what they often say about national tests:

> "The test questions are too hard for our students. And they were written in a way our students could not understand. And our students could not follow the format of the questions."

You will be able to say to teachers:

> "You created these tests yourselves—both the content and the format. We know you didn't make them too hard because you knew that we expected 75 percent [or some such percent] to get them right. We're sure that really unusual questions were filtered out before they got into the pool. As to format, we're confident you chose a format that would be familiar to our students."

Further, you can—and should—say to teachers:

> "You also wrote the 12:00 objectives on which these questions are based. We know you did that with an understanding of what our students could learn. So, since the 12:00 objectives are reasonable and the test questions are reasonable because you wrote them, then poor test results must be caused by something else.

"Perhaps we didn't give you the materials you needed. Perhaps we didn't give you enough time in the school day. Perhaps you didn't understand which teaching methods would work best. Let's figure out what caused the problem and solve it. But we know it wasn't at 12:00 and it wasn't at 9:00."

Disadvantages of Local Tests

If local tests are such a powerful device for producing more student learning, why don't more districts have them? An excellent question. There are probably two reasons:

1. Many teachers and central office administrators do not have the expertise to produce 9:00 local tests without outside help, but many school boards are reluctant to pay for that help.

2. Local tests are expensive. Apart from the expense of creating the pool of test questions, it is also expensive to type, proof, print, distribute, score, analyze, interpret, and use the results of local tests. And it takes a lot of time. National tests are cheaper and speedier. State tests are even more so. It costs school boards both more cash and more administrative positions for local tests.

Of course, no money could be better spent. If you cannot tell what students are learning because you have no clear-cut way to measure or judge your 12:00 objectives, you cannot judge the success of your district.

Spending the money and time to put local tests in place will give you two important benefits:

1. Students will learn more because teachers will teach the 12:00 objectives more effectively when they know there will be 9:00 tests on every one of them.

2. You will be able to tell what students have learned—and not learned—in a clearer, more precise, more usable way than ever before.

National Tests

What is a "national" test, anyway? You can spend a long time on a board not knowing. And little wonder. Here are the basics:

1. Professional eductors *never* call them "national." They always call them "nationally standardized."

2. Most national tests are published by commercial, profit-making companies—just like textbooks.

3. You can buy any national test you wish—just like textbooks.

4. Some textbook companies also publish "national" tests. Those tests are not tied closely to their textbooks. You can buy their books or their tests or both—or neither.

5. You do not have to use any national test.

6. Sometimes a *state* adopts a national test as its *state* test. Then you do have to use it because it has become your *state's* test.

7. The names of national tests are a professional disgrace. The names make it (almost) impossible for a civilian to figure anything out.

   - Some national tests are named for *states*. Iowa Tests of Basic Skills and California Achievement Test are two examples.

   - Some national tests are named for *universities*. Stanford Achievement Test is one example.

   - Some national tests are named for *companies*. Science Research Associates Reading Test is one example.

   - Some national tests are named for *people*. Nelson-Denny, Gates-McGinity, and Seashore are three examples. (Seashore is a person who sounds like a place, adding to the confusion.)

   - Some national tests are named for *public officials*. The President's Physical Fitness Test is one example.

- Some national tests are named for their *subject field*. Degrees of Reading Power is one example.

- Some national tests are named for their *scope*. Comprehensive Tests of Basic Skills is one example.

- Some national tests are named for their *design or function*. Sequential Tests of Educational Progress and School and College Abilities Test are two examples.

- Some national tests are named for *demographic areas*. Metropolitan Achievement Test is one example.

- Some national tests are named for *federal projects*. National Assessment of Educational Progress is one example.

- Some national tests are named for nationally-packaged *school programs*. Advanced Placement Tests is one example.

- Some national tests are named for *organizations*. College Entrance Examination Board Achievement Test in Chemistry is one example.

- Some national tests have nicknames; some don't. Some have acronyms; some don't.

This utter mishmash of names permits professionals to make undecipherable statements like this:

> "We dropped the Iowas in favor of CTBS when we saw our Board scores go down, even though our ACT scores went up along with our AP scores, but we may switch back to ITBS if they don't re-norm STEP because DRP is expensive and SRA is not used much in this state."

How National Tests Are Developed. Let us tell you how national tests are built. Publishing a national test is a commercial venture. Each test publisher surveys what typical districts around the country are teaching and builds a test based on some of the objectives those districts are teaching in common. Publishers do this because such a test will then be salable to the typical school district. You can see that such a method of building a test would keep it from containing unusual content. Thus, what national tests contain are usually the most common and most basic things students are taught in school.

If your teachers or administrators tell you that the national test you now use contains many things that your schools do not teach, you should say to them, "What does this district know that the rest of the country doesn't? Or, what do they know that we don't?" To put it plainly, there are few good reasons for not teaching what national tests test, inasmuch as national tests test the basic, commonly-taught objectives. They are, if you will, minimum tests for the nation.

How Your Local Objectives Should Relate to a National Test. Your local curriculum should be much larger than any national test—larger than all national tests combined. Accordingly, your students should be able to score well on almost *any* national test—not only the one you are using now.

If you draw a picture of your objectives and the objectives covered by say five different national tests, it should look something like this:

Your objectives

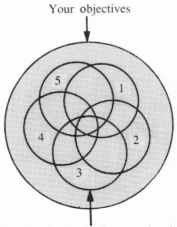

Objectives for five different national tests

A national test may cover no more than perhaps 30 percent of the English, mathematics, science, and social studies you teach in a typical grade. The better your local curriculum, the less of it will be covered by a national test. If you teach only what is on the national test, you are not teaching much.

Your district is probably already using one of the national tests and has been for some years. In picking whatever national test you now use, your administrators and teachers should have looked carefully at the objectives behind the questions to see whether they were contained in your own objectives at 12:00.

If that was not done when your district chose its national test, it should be done now in order to eliminate a favorite explanation for poor test performance (as discussed earlier): "The national test we use contains things we do not teach here in our district."

In working with districts, we always have teachers look inside whatever national test their district is now using, make sure the objectives behind those national test questions are *included* in their district's 12:00 list of objectives, and designate them with asterisks. Board members, administrators, teachers, and parents are then able to see at a glance which local objectives are being tested on the national test. Everyone can then work hard to make sure students learn those objectives. Will this improve national test scores? Of course it will. Will this improve student learning—a much more important question? Of course it will.

By the way, this is not "teaching to the test." We are not, of course, suggesting that teachers teach students the *answers to the questions* in the national test. What we are saying is that students should be taught all the *objectives* on which those national test questions are based. That's only fair.

How National Tests Are Scored. Every national test has been given to a representative national sample of students—probably in the year before it was published. The conditions under which the test was given were very carefully controlled—that is, "standardized"—so that scores would be comparable from one place to another.

To get comparable scores for your students, you must give the test under the standard conditions described in the instructions: Use the same directions, limit students to the same amount of time, give them no hints, and so on. The standard national scoring yardstick and the standard testing conditions are what make the test "nationally standardized." You can use it to see how your students rate against other students nationwide—but only if you give it to your students under the same carefully controlled conditions.

When the publisher gave the test to a national sample of students (every publisher picks its own national sample of students, incidentally, and no two publishers have ever used the same sample of students), it yielded as expected some low scores, some average scores, and some high scores. Those scores were converted into a standard scale for judging all future test scores. For example, the score made by the average student in the sample became the score designated as the 50th national percentile for all future users of the test.

Those original scores are still the standard yardstick for measuring the performance of your students on that particular test today—even if the original scores date from, say, 1977. Today's scores in your district are not compared to *today's* scores in *other* districts, but to the *original* scores in *other* districts. So if you give a test this year, your results will not be compared to the results of other districts that also gave the same test this year. The publisher will go on using the original scoring scale until a new, revised "edition" of the test is developed and used with a new national sample of students.

Typically, a test publisher will issue two "forms" of the same edition of the test at one time. The two forms test the same objectives with different, but equivalent, questions. This allows schools to switch between the two forms every year or so in order to keep students and teachers from becoming unduly familiar with the identical test year after year.

When Is It Time To Change to Another National Test? The only legitimate reason for changing the national test you are now using is if your 12:00 objectives no longer match the objectives on which your national test is based. Such a mismatch can occur only when you change your objectives radically or the publisher makes an extraordinary revision in its national test.

Once you have established your 12:00 objectives, as we said at 12:00, they should remain quite stable. You will make a change here and a change there, but 90 percent of the objectives could—and should—remain unchanged for years.

National tests themselves are not changed very often either. About every seven to ten years, the test publisher may come out with a revised "edition" of the test. This is a market-driven decision. Does the publisher need to come up with a new "model" to appeal to the buyers? If so, the new edition of the test, like a new edition of a familiar textbook, will have changes. It will have some— perhaps all—new questions and perhaps some alteration in the objectives tested. But even then, many of the objectives would understandably remain the same, inasmuch as elementary and secondary curriculum does not change much—even in 10 years.

What a test publisher does do when creating a new edition of the test is to "re-norm" the test. This means that the publisher once again gives the test—this time, the revised test—to a large, carefully drawn sample of students nationwide and then uses their scores to decide the scale for scoring that test in the future.

Again, the score made by the average student in the sample is designated as the 50th national percentile for all future users of the test. You can see that if students nationwide get higher scores than 10 years ago, the average score moves up and thus the score your students need in order to earn the 50th percentile gets higher. On the other hand, if students nationwide get lower scores than 10 years ago, the average score moves down and your students can reach the 50th percentile with lower scores. Thus, when tests are "re-normed" and you decide to buy the new edition rather than sticking with the old edition, it is likely that your test scores will go up automatically if students across the country are getting worse or that your scores will go down automatically if students across the country are getting better—even though your students have not changed at all. When you change national tests to a newer edition, be sure to ask the test publisher for a statement about what change in your scores you should expect because of the re-norming of that new edition. The change could be as much as 5 to 20 points, but your teachers should receive neither credit nor blame for a difference caused by re-norming.

We advise, in most cases, not to change your national test if you can help it. In that way, you will have a consistent yardstick against which to measure the achievement of your students over time. Breaking your yardstick by changing either the edition of your test or by changing from one brand of national test to another will make it difficult or impossible for you to get a firm grasp on whether your students are doing better or worse from one year to the next. And that, in turn, makes it difficult or impossible to know whether changes made by the superintendent at 3:00 or 6:00 worked.

Which Grades To Test? Most districts use a national test only in a sample of grades—say 3, 6, and 9—to get a sense of how they are doing overall. That saves money, but it does not sufficiently pinpoint grade levels where you are relatively weak. Thus, you cannot take corrective action with a rifle; you have to use a shotgun.

If you want to improve student learning as well as evaluate it, we recommend that you use a national test in every grade. However, if you use a local test in every grade, you can locate weak grades with that and use a national test only in selected grades to see how you compare to the nation overall. That's another advantage of a local test: It can cut the cost of a national test.

Which Subjects To Test? Most districts use a national test only in a few subjects—usually English and math, sometimes social studies, occasionally science, almost never foreign languages, art, music, vocational education, or anything else. Boards (more likely, superintendents) act as if they believe that:

- English and math are the only subjects worth testing. (We say any subject worth teaching is worth testing.)

- If test scores are satisfactory in English and math, learning is satisfactory in other subjects. (We say maybe so, maybe not.)

- English and math are the only subjects they can afford to test. (We say if you can afford only two, test

English and math this year, social studies and science next year, and two other subjects every year until you sweep the spotlight over the whole curriculum. Then, start again with English and math.)

(You could use this same technique as a way to sweep the spotlight over all *grades* as well.)

If you want to improve learning in all subjects as well as evaluate it, we recommend that you use a national test in every subject. (They will be much harder to find in the non-academic subjects, but have your administrators keep looking.) Here again, if you use a local test in every subject, you can identify weaknesses with that and use a national test only in selected subjects (different ones every year) to see how you are doing overall.

Getting Test Score Reports. Someone has to score your national tests. Scoring can be done by the company that publishes the tests (most sell a test-scoring service), by some other organization that sells such a service, or by your own school district (if it is large enough to justify buying the scoring equipment). Deciding who does the scoring is minor. What is major is deciding who gets the reports of the results and what the reports will contain.

There are several audiences for test results:

- You
- The superintendent
- The superintendent's staff
- Principals
- Teachers
- Parents
- Students

Ideally, reports should differ for each audience. Students, parents, and teachers can benefit from objective-by-objective results for each student: Can Mary do two-column addition? Can Jon use semicolons? Can Mark read political maps? Can Jay interpret graphs? Such reports can guide corrective action objective by objective and student by student.

Principals can use objective-by-objective results for each elementary classroom and each high school "section" (Mr. Jordan's second period German class, for example).

The superintendent and his or her staff can use objective-by-objective results for each school.

The board can use results for the district as a whole—and perhaps school by school. We recommend that the board get results objective by objective; you will understand better what is happening and your conversations with your administrators will be much more substantial.

Advantages of National Tests

The major advantage is that you can tell where you stand in the nation. No other test can tell you that.

No matter how good you believe your objectives are, no matter how high your local test scores are, and no matter how high your state test scores are, you should know how you stand in the nation.

Disadvantages of National Tests

The only real disadvantage to national tests is that they cost money. But, since there is no cheaper way to learn what they tell you, we would say that it is money well spent.

Critics of national tests cite many disadvantages, including all of those listed earlier in this chapter. Having read this chapter, perhaps you can now respond better to those typical criticisms. None of them is good enough to keep you from using national test results to help you judge the success of your district.

Among the most likely critics will be your own testing director, if you have one. In listening to countless reports of national test scores given by local testing directors to school boards, we have found out two things:

1. Testing directors seem to be more expert at "explaining away" the results than at explaining the results. Many focus their presentations on reasons for not believing the results and, therefore, for not using the results.

2. We can almost never understand the testing directors' reports—either written or oral. And neither can you. What puzzles us is why school boards put up with such poorly conceived and poorly presented reports of such critical information. Board members almost never ask questions about the reports—or at least almost never pursue their questions long enough to get them truly answered.

You can solve these two problems by asking your testing director (or whoever supplies your test reports) to give you nothing but the *national percentile* for each subject you test (including a breakdown by "subtest"—such as reading comprehension within English—and by objective, if available) in each grade you test—for the district as a whole and for each separate school. National percentiles are the simplest statistic for you to understand. The scale runs from 1 to 99 with the average at 50. You can interpret 25 as being pretty poor and 75 as being pretty good, depending on the quality of the raw material you get as students (more about that in the 10:30 chapter). National percentiles will give you the clearest overall view of how well your students are doing compared to other students across the country.

Please ask questions about your national test results and insist they be answered. No other information you get is more important. If you cannot understand the test results, we believe the chances are excellent that your administrators and teachers cannot understand them either. Keep asking questions. Insist that the reports be improved. You must have this information to govern the schools.

Recently, we met with a school board in the state of Washington. The board's president was an intelligent and articulate attorney with some years of experience on the board. There were about 25 people in the room—the board, the superintendent, and the central administrative staff, including the testing director. We were talking about the board's responsibility for 9:00. The president interrupted, looked at the testing director, and said:

> "George, in all my years on the board, I have never been able to understand any of your reports. I read them; I listen to you talk; I ask a few questions; then I give up. The only thing I can understand is that you think that measuring student learning at 9:00 is very complex, that national tests have a lot of limitations, and that we cannot do anything with the results."

He could have been speaking for almost any board, almost anywhere in this country.

The clock changes all that. The idea of 9:00 is simple enough for every civilian board member to understand. What you must ask for as proof of success at 9:00 is a report of how well your students learned each objective you put at 12:00. Such a report would give the Washington attorney what he has been missing in all his years on the board.

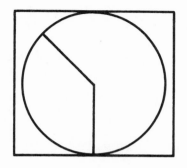

10:30   Setting Standards

Do not look at test results if you have not set standards for judging them. It's pointless to examine learning if you don't know how good the learning should be. You won't know whether to laugh, smile, frown, or cry.

If students scored at the 65th national percentile, one board would terminate the superintendent's contract, while another would beg the superintendent to accept a three-year extension. Both boards have standards. They know what they want. Do you?

We placed this discussion of standards at 10:30 because that is the point of comparison between what you ordered at 12:00 and what you got at 9:00.

Whatever method you choose for setting learning standards at 10:30, here are two important things to remember:

1. Board members must set the learning standards and not leave it to the administrators and teachers.

2. Board members should expect learning to improve and should, therefore, set higher learning standards each year.

Setting Standards as a Technique for Improving Learning

Why is it so important for civilians, instead of professionals, to set learning standards? Because if you expect more, you will get more. In all of our experience, we have never seen a case where administrators and teachers believed that students could learn as much as school board members believed they could learn.

You will set higher standards for students than your professional staff would. It is not hard to see why administrators and teachers would consciously or subconsciously underestimate how well their students could do. Lower standards are easier to meet.

Not long ago we were talking with the superintendent of one of the nation's largest school districts about improving learning. The superintendent said:

> "You know what our district is like—poor, disadvantaged, black. We have finally gotten up to the 50th national percentile. We are proud of that. It was hard work. Took years. We got wonderful editorials in our newspapers congratulating us. Do we need to do better than the 50th percentile? Not in this district, we don't. We feel very lucky to have gotten this far. We're settling."

We don't believe many school board members would have agreed with that professional assessment of how much achievement to expect from students. We'll bet that superintendent's board of education would not have settled. And we'll bet yours wouldn't, either.

That brings us to the second point. The chances are good that if those students could get to the 50th percentile, they could do even better with even harder work. It is not necessary to settle for the learning you are now getting—even if it is pretty good. The kinds of people we would like to see setting learning standards at 10:30 are the kinds of people who say:

> "We know we're at the 95th percentile on the national test we are using now. We probably would be on any national test we could give. But somehow we feel that our students can do even better than that. Look at the raw material we give you professionals to work with. How about the 98th?"

That's the way school board members in one great Midwest suburban district talked to their administrators when we sat with them a couple of years ago. That's the way you should talk when you want to improve learning. Don't settle; set higher standards.

In many stories we have heard and from our own work in school districts, we have seen that the most common result of setting learning standards is that the school district exceeds the standards it has set. Why that happens is quite evident. In trying to reach the standards, everyone works so hard that student achievement surpasses them. Students work harder in class and at home. Teachers teach more purposefully and perhaps even more creatively. Administrators run the schools more efficiently and effectively. School board members try harder to give the schools the financial support they need. Parents take more interest in the schools generally and in their children's learning specifically. And it works.

So, think hard about what those learning standards should be for your district, set them, and wait for the good news.

Measuring Ability Before Setting Standards

When setting 10:30 standards for learning, you may find yourselves as board members discussing just how bright your students are. You want them to learn up to their potential, of course. But what is their potential? How much *ability* do they have to produce the *achievement* you are calling for?

If the distinction between *ability* and *achievement* is a bit fuzzy for you, let's take a minute to sharpen the focus. Professionals use the word *ability* to mean what a student *might learn* (if he or she tried hard). The synonyms for *ability* are *capability*, *capacity*, *possibility*, *po-*

tential learning, and other such words. All of them mean what a barrel *could* hold—not what it holds now. Professionals use the word *achievement* to mean what a student has *already learned* (whether he or she has tried hard or not). The synonyms for *achievement* are *accomplishment*, *past performance*, *track record*, *actual learning*, and other such words. All of them mean what a barrel holds *now*—not what it could hold.

You have to make that distinction before you can set standards. You must set standards by estimating ability, not by judging achievement. How much ability do your students have? Let us tell you how one district answered that question so that it could set realistically high standards for its students on national tests.

One night at a school board meeting not far from Chicago, the school board president said to us:

> "Here is a chart showing our results on a national test. As you can see, our first graders start off at about the 75th national percentile in English and math. By the time they get to twelfth grade, we manage to bring them all the way down to the 25th national percentile."

Here was the chart they showed us for mathematics:

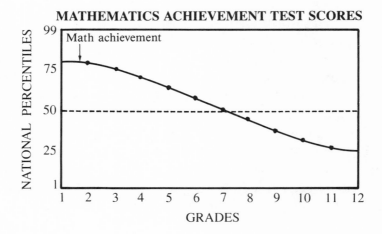

MATHEMATICS ACHIEVEMENT TEST SCORES

One of the board members followed up by saying:

"Now, I don't know much about testing. But I am an engineer, and I can extrapolate that downward slope. I say: Thank God they graduate. Five more years here and they would know nothing."

In that district, the school board president had a real knack for asking good questions. He said to the superintendent:

"Do you like it here?"

We believe that in time the superintendent said to each principal:

"Do you like being the principal in your school?"

And then the principals said to the teachers:

"Do you like teaching in this school?"

And finally, we believe the teachers said to the students:

"You're making me look bad."

Rising expectations for students began to turn that district around. Nothing was more important than that. Expect more; you'll probably get it. Don't, and you certainly won't.

We began our work in that district by asking everyone we could find what he or she did with the national test results every year. The board members said:

"We feel bad about them. But, of course, we can't really do anything about the results ourselves as board members. We look to the superintendent to correct the problem."

The superintendent said:

"Well, I feel bad. But, after all, I'm not on the firing line out there in the schools. I really have to trust the principals to turn the situation around."

The principals each said something like:

"I feel bad when I get the results. But, of course, I'm not teaching the children myself. I have to rely on classroom teachers to fix this problem."

And finally, we asked some of the teachers, who said something like:

"The school board has some reason for giving these national tests. We really don't know what it is. We're not sure the tests are any good. So we just file the results away and wait for next year."

It was clear that no one in the district was using the test results. No one analyzed them, interpreted them, and tried to figure out what they showed about weaknesses in the district curriculum. "Feel bad and file" was all they did. You already know that is not enough.

In meetings with teachers, we asked them to explain the decline in achievement between grades 1 and 12. They told us that their students got dumber every year. We laughed and laughed. They said to us:

"No, we really mean it. You see, every time we get a pretty good family here in our district with some pretty bright kids, the family gets transferred out of the Chicago area and off to the home office in New York or Los Angeles. Mayflower rolls up and takes the good family away, and you should see what Allied Van Lines brings in as a replacement. We have severe brain drain from our district. Most of the families with bright kids leave by the time the kids are old enough to start middle school. That's why the test scores go down."

"You can't prove that," we said.

"Yes, we can," they said. "Here are the scores from the ability test we give to all of our students."

Here is the chart they showed us, with the ability line added to the achievement line:

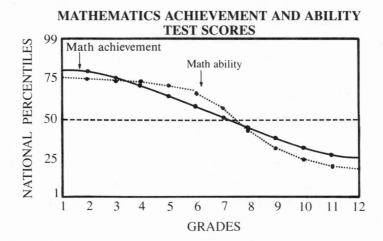

MATHEMATICS ACHIEVEMENT AND ABILITY TEST SCORES

It was amazing. The ability test scores were virtually indistinguishable from the achievement test scores. They both started at about the 75th percentile in grade 1 and wound up at about the 25th percentile in grade 12. Principals and teachers used these ability scores to justify their belief that students were learning as much as they could. If they pushed these students any harder, expected any more from them, the students might collapse under the pressure. Students were doing the best they could with the raw ability they had. The district was living up to its philosophy statement (the same philosophy statement that all 16,000 school districts have): "We believe that every student should realize his or her full potential."

This meant, of course, that the learning in that district could not be improved. Those teachers were getting all the juice out of the oranges. If they squeezed any harder, the students might have nervous breakdowns, but they would not be able to learn any more.

So, the students were getting dumber every year— just as the teachers had told us. The achievement scores

went down with the ability scores. They were alike—
exactly alike.

In fact, they were so much alike that we began to get
suspicious. We looked harder at the results from the two
prominent national tests, both produced by the same
publisher. Then we did something we had never done before. We looked inside the tests.

We pulled out a page of questions from the achievement test and a page of questions from the ability test.
We handed out the two pages to groups of teachers and
administrators in that district. (We have since handed out
those pages to thousands of teachers, principals, superintendents, and board members in various workshops we
have conducted around the country.) We asked the teachers and administrators to hold up the page from the ability test. Half of them held up one page, and half of them
held up the other page. They could not tell the difference
between the two tests. Neither can our audiences today.
Neither can we. Neither could the students in that district, we hypothesized, which is why they got the same
scores on both tests.

In other words, those two tests produced by the same
test publisher were measuring the same thing. Small wonder the test scores were the same. We wondered, "Is ability dragging down achievement—or is achievement
dragging down ability?"

There was only one way to find out. We needed an
independent test of ability—one not connected with the
current achievement test the district used, one not published by the same testing company. We reached for a
popular, group-administered, paper-and-pencil ability
test published by another company and gave it to students in grades 1, 3, 5, 8, and 11. Then we plotted the
results. Here they are:

MATHEMATICS ACHIEVEMENT AND MATHEMATICS ABILITY TEST SCORES AND GENERAL ABILITY TEST SCORES

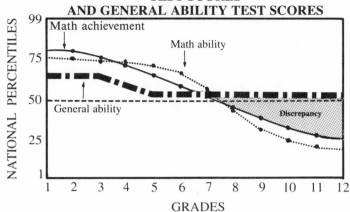

That downward ability slope was essentially gone. The independent ability test showed that students in that district were above average in ability in grades 1 through 3 and average in ability in grades 5 through 11.

What a useful discrepancy that produced between their ability and their achievement in the secondary schools. For the first time, board members could say, "We know our secondary school students can do better than they're doing. Now make their achievement match their ability." If you don't have a discrepancy between ability and achievement based on something—a measure or a belief—you cannot raise achievement.

Even so, the independent ability test indicated that something strange was happening between grades 3 and 5: a sharp drop in ability. Too early for puberty—a favorite scapegoat. But what could it be? So we did it again. We opened up the third grade test and the fifth grade test, took a page of questions from each, and handed out those pages to various audiences. This time they could tell the difference.

The ability test was a *picture* test in grade 3, but a *reading* test in grade 5. We said:

> "Your students can show their intelligence with pictures, but they can't show it with words. They can perhaps *draw* their intelligence, or maybe even *dance* it for you—but they cannot *read* their intelligence to you. Possibly if you taught them to read better, they would look (or be?) more intelligent. Then you could teach them something else."

The social studies department chairperson in the high school announced at our next meeting with the teachers that he felt there must be a way to find out once and for all just how bright the students really were. He wanted that question answered definitively for students across all the grades.

> *He*: Surely, there is a picture test we could give to all of the students—even the high school students—to see just how bright they really are. How about a picture test for everybody?
>
> *We*: That is a ridiculous idea. You would never give a picture test to high school students. Nothing like that even exists. Forget it.
>
> *He*: But surely there must be something?
>
> *We*: No. There isn't. Well, there is the Stanford-Binet and there is the Wechsler Intelligence Scales for Children. Those are two ability tests that don't require students to read. But we only use those on special kids—either very bright kids or very slow kids. The Binet and the Wechsler are individually administered. They take about an hour and a half to give to each student. No district ever uses these tests to judge the ability of their regular students. It's too expensive.
>
> *He*: Are they any good?
>
> *We*: They are the best we have in the profession. But, you would never use them for regular kids.

He: Let's do it. We ought to find out—once and for all. Let's use them with regular kids.

We: That's a ridiculous idea.

About a month later, we came back to the school board and said:

"We have come up with a great idea. Let's give the Wechsler to a random sample of *all* your students in grades 1, 3, 5, 8, and 11—including the *regular* kids. Let's see once and for all just how bright your students really are."

The board agreed with our (well, his) ingenious idea. The district brought in a team of eight outside psychologists and gave individually-administered Wechsler IQ tests across the five grades to a large sample of regular students. The results looked like this:

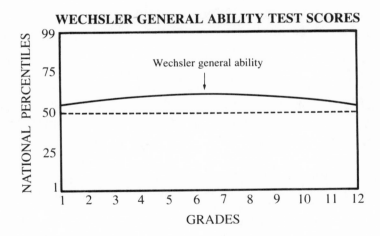

The students were slightly above average in ability right across all of the grades—from 1 through 11. The downward ability slope was gone—for good.

Now the board knew that its students could learn more. The discrepancy between ability and achievement was substantial, starting in the late elementary grades. Teachers could no longer say that they were getting all the juice out of the oranges. They knew they had to squeeze harder, and they did. The results over the next decade in that district were amazing.

The district continued using the group-administered, paper-and-pencil ability test year after year as a low-cost independent measure of ability. As student achievement scores increased year after year, those independent ability test scores also increased. That is, as students were taught to read better and better, they appeared to get more and more intelligent. In fact, the ability test scores always kept a little ahead of the achievement test scores— preserving an extremely useful discrepancy between ability and achievement. Since students were never quite learning up to their ability, they could always be expected to learn even more.

We had an occasion not long ago to repeat the experiment in entirely different circumstances. We were working in a city in the Southeast with disappointingly low achievement. We could not tell at first what was more depressed—their achievement or their spirit. Administrators told us privately:

> "We have been ravaged by Court-ordered desegregation and by white flight. The good students have, quite frankly, all gone. We are 70 percent black; we are poor; we are a city of broken homes and semi-literate parents. We have the students achieving at the 35th national percentile, and we are surprised we can do that well."

Fortunately, the brand new superintendent did not buy that. He believed in his heart that the district's poor black students could learn, but he also believed that they would not learn as long as their teachers and principals believed they could not.

Copying the idea that the chairman of the high school social studies department had given us, we persuaded the superintendent to bring in a team of psychologists. In a deliberate move to add credibility, he brought them in from a very prominent university. The psychologists gave the Wechsler to a random sample of regular students throughout the district—kindergarten through grade 12. The results were as the superintendent had believed—or hoped—they would be. The team of psychologists declared that the students were average in ability—at about the 50th national percentile. Local newspapers echoed that declaration in blazing headlines. That gave the superintendent the discrepancy he needed: 50th national percentile in ability; 35th national percentile in achievement.

Further, it gave the teachers in the city new hope. Maybe their students could learn more. Parents, some of them anyway, raised their hopes—and their expectations. For the first time in years, people inside and outside of the schools began to believe that students in that big, poor city could learn.

Actually, they had more reason for hope than even the Wechsler test scores showed. The Wechsler contains 10 subtests. Some of those subtests are closely related to and highly influenced by what students are taught in school; the others are more closely related to raw intelligence and are less influenced by classroom learning. A detailed analysis of the Wechsler results showed that the students did significantly better on the subtests of raw intelligence. That enabled us to say to the teachers:

> "If you would teach them more, they would be smarter. Their intelligence scores, even on the Wechsler, are being depressed by the fact that they have not been taught enough in school."

You need to know how smart your students are. You need to know whether their ability puts them at the 30th national percentile, the 50th national percentile, or the 80th national percentile. Until you know how smart they are, you will not be able to set realistically high learning standards for them. Your students may be smarter than your teachers and administrators think. You ought to find out.

Setting Standards for National Tests

Ability testing of your students is one way to help school board members set realistically high learning standards for students. Of course, that is just one method. Some school boards feel perfectly capable of setting learning standards based on their common sense and their experience with students in the school district— without ability testing.

One brave Virginia school board looked back at the past, thought ahead to the future, and said:

> "Five years from now, we want out students to be at the 75th national percentile in English and math in the elementary grades and at the 60th national percentile in the secondary grades."

What's so high about those standards, you might ask? The day the school board made that statement, the students were at about the 50th national percentile in the elementary grades and about the 40th national percentile in the secondary grades. The five-year target was ambitious for that board. But a board member said:

> "We've come pretty far in the last five years, and we're proud of it. But we're not going to stop here. We believe our students can do more, and we're willing to give our schools the money and support they need to do it. We know we're going to need to recruit great teachers to move the kids 20 or 25 national percentile points. So, we're aiming to have the highest paid teach-

ers in the state. We're putting up the money to meet our standards."

The initiative for setting those learning standards in that Virginia district came directly from the board members. It did not come from the administrators, who had already done a good job. But the board was not settling.

A second story comes from a school district farther south, where we were working with an unusually aggressive, intelligent superintendent. We gave him an idea his board should have had in its 10:30 territory, but didn't.

The week before school opened one August, the superintendent called his 50 principals to a workshop. He said:

"Here are the results from the national achievement test we gave in your building last May—plotted on graphs by grade level. Each graph shows the achievement test scores for your school on each subtest—vocabulary, math computation, reading comprehension, and so on. Please plot your test scores for next year."

A typical graph looked like this:

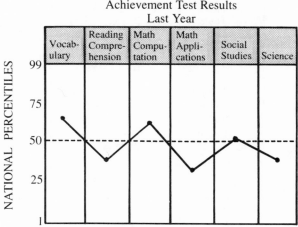

WILLARD ELEMENTARY – GRADE 4
Achievement Test Results
Last Year

A conversation with one principal ensued:

Principal: I must have misunderstood you. How can we plot the results for next year when the students haven't taken the tests yet?

Superintendent: I'm looking for promises. I want you to think hard about the students you have, the teachers you have, and what you accomplished last year. Then I want you to promise me the most learning you can for next year. I'm looking for more learning in each school.

Principal: But I can't do that without talking to my teachers first.

Superintendent: Have you heard of the idea of principals as instructional leaders, Rosa? I want you to talk with your teachers right after you promise me the test scores for next year.

It was not easy for the principals to draw these "promise lines." The results showed several different patterns.

Some principals' lines looked like this:

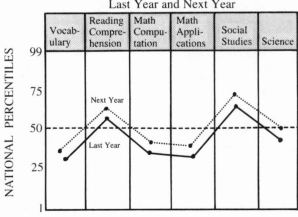

SCHOOL A – GRADE 4
Last Year and Next Year

They were saying, "I'll promise just a little bit more learning everywhere." The superintendent was not impressed.

Some principals' lines looked like this:

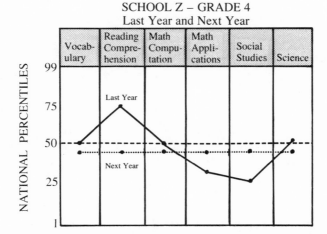

They were saying, "I'll give you some there, but I'm going to take it back here." The superintendent was not impressed.

Some principals' lines looked like this:

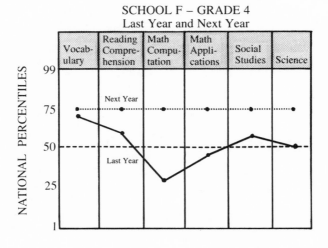

They were saying, "If my students can learn that much vocabulary, I'll bet they can do it in math computation, too." The superintendent was impressed. He went on to bargain with the other principals for more learning before he accepted their promises.

He then collected the "promise lines," studied them, averaged them for the entire district, and made his own promise to the school board. He said, "I'm going to give you 5 more national percentile points next May—districtwide."

What a back-to-school story that made for the local newspapers! But all year long, the superintendent worried about whether he could keep his promise. Constructive worry, we would call it—the kind of worry that improves learning.

What happened the next May? He made good on his promise—by double. Instead of 5 national percentile points, he gave the school board 10. The school district had tried so hard to keep his promise to the school board and to the newspaper-reading public that it had exceeded his expectations. That's the way it usually works. Promise more, you'll do more. Maybe much more.

If you haven't collected "promise lines" from your superintendent and if your superintendent has not collected them from your principals, you are missing a great way to set learning standards at 10:30—and get them met.

Setting Standards for Local Tests

As we explained in the 9:00 chapter, the national tests that you are using test only a portion of the many 12:00 objectives you adopted. How can you set learning standards at 10:30 to cover *all* of your 12:00 objectives? After all, you are measuring all of them at 9:00; therefore, you must have some learning standards for judging those 9:00 results at 10:30.

One simple way to set those standards is to adopt what you told the teachers at 12:00 when they were writing the objectives for you: Write the objectives so that 75 percent (or 80 percent or 70 percent or whatever you said) of your students can learn them and remember them. When you said that at 12:00, you were actually setting your 10:30 learning standard. When the superintendent gives you the objective-by-objective results at 9:00, you can simply look to see what percent of your students learned each one. You will be looking for numbers of 75 (or 80 or 70 or whatever you said) and higher. That's how you can review the scores on each of your 12:00 objectives according to your 10:30 learning standard.

Of course, you could apply graduated standards on a time schedule, especially if the new objectives you adopted were a lot tougher than the old ones, or if you had had none at all until now. You could create a table like this:

Year	Percent of Students Expected To Learn Each Objective
Year 1	60
Year 2	65
Year 3	70

The table could differ by grade and by subject, of course.

Closing the Circle

You can adjourn at 10:30. Your work is done. You have set the learning goals and objectives at 12:00, called for the measurement results for each objective at 9:00, and judged those results against the 10:30 learning standards you set. There is nothing more for you to do—and there is nothing more important for you to do.

So don't go home until you've done it.

Index